# TAMBO AND BONES

LONDON :
CAMBRIDGE UNIVERSITY PRESS

———

NEW YORK :
G. E. STECHERT & COMPANY

TOKYO :
MARUZEN AND COMPANY, LTD.

SHANGHAI :
EDWARD EVANS & SONS, LTD.

MANILA :
PHILIPPINE EDUCATION CO.

BUENOS AIRES :
J. LAJOUANE & COMPANY

# TAMBO AND BONES

*A History of the American Minstrel Stage*

BY

CARL WITTKE, Ph.D.
*Professor of History*
*The Ohio State University*

DURHAM · NORTH CAROLINA
DUKE UNIVERSITY PRESS
1930

TO

# WALTER E. SMITH
## IN MEMORIAM

*"Go in, brack man, de day's yo' own."*

# PREFACE

The minstrel show was a unique development, a purely native form of entertainment, and a distinctively American contribution to theatrical history. Whatever interest this little volume may have for the general reader, it is my hope that it will be received as a serious contribution to American social history and to the history of the stage in the United States.

This study was inspired by more than a professional interest in social history. Happy memories of the burnt cork semi-circle, gathered during barnstorming student days, are responsible for an abiding interest and a real love for the old-time minstrel show.

CARL WITTKE

Columbus, Ohio
June 1, 1930

# TABLE OF CONTENTS

# TAMBO AND BONES

# CHAPTER I

## THE ORIGINS OF NEGRO MINSTRELSY

Without negro slavery, the United States would have been deprived of perhaps the only and, certainly, the most considerable body of song sprung from the soil, which properly can be called American folkmusic. And without the large Negro population of the Southern states, the one purely native form of entertainment and the only distinctively American contribution to the theatre—the Negro minstrel show—would have been equally impossible. Music lovers the world over in recent years have found in the negro spirituals and in the songs of plantation days a type of music which is not only intriguingly and often whimsically beautiful, but also worthy of serious study because of its peculiar rhythmic form, its structure, and the unique themes which have been utilized as the *motifs* for more pretentious compositions.

Here is a music which voices the joys and the sorrows, the longing, the fatalism, the aspirations and the sufferings of one of the most musically-gifted peoples of the earth. The Negro has a real sense of rhythm, an ability to improvise as well as to borrow, and a background of deep emotionalism; these qualities, coupled with life in a new environment as the slaves of another race, are the elements

from which genuine American Negro music has
sprung. "Nowhere save on the plantations of the
South," writes one of America's most distinguished
critics, "could the emotional life which is essential to
the development of true folksong be developed. . . ."[1]
The best of the Negro spirituals were born in "a
slave era when heartstrings were taut."[2] They
are exquisite, musical emotionalism, woven on "a
background of torch-lit groves, swaying bodies and
half-closed eyes." But all negro music, whether
spirituals or not, has its appealing qualities. Perhaps even the so-called "barber shop chord," famous
for its close harmony and followed as a model by
many American musicians in arranging songs for
four male voices, had its origin in the days when
white barber shops were unknown in the South.
Every little shop had its quartette of Negro boys or
men who spent their leisure moments, when they
were not serving the tonsorial needs of the master
class, with the guitar and their heaven-given voices.
By some stroke of Providence wherever four Negroes assembled, they almost always managed to
make a quartette, "harmonizing" the old familiar
melodies.[3]

[1] Henry E. Krehbiel, *Afro-American Folksongs* (New York, 1914).

[2] William A. Fisher, *Seventy Negro Spirituals* (Boston, 1926). See Introduction.

[3] See the interesting introduction by James Weldon Johnson, in *The Book of American Negro Spirituals,* compiled by J. R. Johnson and Lawrence Brown (New York, 1925).

The source of Negro minstrelsy is to be found in the soil of the Southland. The troubadours of the American burnt cork circle were utterly different from the minstrels of other lands and earlier times. There was little in the American minstrel show even remotely suggestive of the troubadours, *minnesingers, jongleurs* and bards of medieval Europe, except perhaps a genuine love for song and a common gift of improvising endless verses. The theme of the American performer generally was quite different from that of his European predecessors. All minstrels, to be sure, have sung of lovable eyes and faithful hearts and the mist of moonlight evenings, but the repertory of the blackface minstrel included so many additional themes that minstrelsy became a distinctive American institution. The burnt cork artist of the United States of the nineteenth century could have originated in no other country in the world. His art was indigenous to the United States, and from here it was introduced, with only moderate success, to England, the Continent of Europe, and to other parts of the globe. If it did not flourish elsewhere as it did in the United States, the primary reason was that foreigners could not understand or fully appreciate the peculiarly American conditions from which this entirely new form of entertainment had sprung.[4]

[4] See an excellent article by Brander Matthews, "The Rise and Fall of Negro Minstrelsy," in *Scribner's Magazine*, LVII, 754-759.

The origin of American minstrelsy may be found in the singing and dancing of the slaves of the Southern plantations of ante-bellum days; at least this may be considered its prototype. Slave captains sometimes forced their black cargoes to dance and sing on shipboard on the way across the Atlantic from Africa, and plantation owners in America kept their Negroes happy and productive in the same way. Until recent times it has been customary to pay the song leader of a gang of Negro laborers an extra sum, on the theory that singing added to the effectiveness of the workmen.[5] Often in ante-bellum days the master, in quest of amusement and entertainment, summoned those of his slaves who were specially gifted as singers or dancers to perform for him at the Great House, and on occasion he invited his guests and friends to the performance. More often the Negroes danced and sang because of their own innate and irrepressible fondness for rhythmic and musical expression. As early as 1784, Thomas Jefferson, in his famous *Notes on the State of Virginia,* described "the banjar," which the slaves had brought with them from Africa and which the Sage of Monticello believed to be the "origin of the guitar." The crooning melodies sung to the accompaniment of guitar or banjo by the plantation blacks, and their peculiar shuffling dances, were the models

[5] Newman I. White, *American Negro Folk-Songs* (Cambridge, 1928), pp. 5-7.

upon which the first blackface performers patterned their acts. These Negro performances were spontaneous and almost instinctive. In more recent times, some of the chain gangs of Negro prisoners working on Southern roads, still fall quite automatically into singing while they work; the "end men" on the chain develop a real talent for improvising new stanzas, while the others chant the chorus, swinging their picks and tossing them around with a dexterity that suggests the skill of the professional minstrel end man with his tambourines or bones. From the pathos and humor of the Negroes, their superstitions and their religious fervor, their plaintive and their hilarious melodies, their peculiarities of manner, dress and speech, the white minstrel built his performance.[6]

The genuine darky has been depicted as "the folk-figure of a simple, somewhat rustic character, instinctively humorous, irrationally credulous, gifted in song and dance, interesting in spontaneous frolic, endowed with artless philosophy."[7] In the process of adapting this type to the theatre, the stage Negro

[6] See Dailey Paskman and Sigmund Spaeth, *Gentlemen, Be Seated! A Parade of the Old-Time Minstrels* (Garden City, New York, 1928), p. 176. The most valuable part of this work is the pictures, words, and music of early minstrel performances which the authors have diligently collected and accurately reprinted. The historical account is very brief and admittedly inadequate.

[7] Francis Pendleton Gaines, *The Southern Plantation: A Study in the Development and Accuracy of a Tradition* (New York, 1925), p. 3.

became quite a different person from the model on which he was formed. More specifically, the plantation type which got into minstrelsy apparently was calculated to give the impression that all Negroes were lazy, shiftless fellows, careless of the morrow. The stage Negro loved watermelons and ate them in a peculiar way. He turned out to be an expert wielder of the razor, a weapon which he always had ready for use on such special social occasions as crap games, of which the stage Negro was passionately fond.

In minstrelsy, the Negro type had all these characteristics and many more. He always was distinguished by an unusually large mouth and a peculiar kind of broad grin; he dressed in gaudy colors and in a flashy style; he usually consumed more gin than he could properly hold; and he loved chickens so well that he could not pass a chicken-coop without falling into temptation. In minstrelsy, moreover, the Negro's alleged love for the grand manner led him to use words so long that he not only did not understand their meaning, but twisted the syllables in the most ludicrous fashion in his futile efforts to pronounce them. This, in the main, was the Negro of the joke-book tradition and more especially of the minstrel tradition, and undoubtedly he was a somewhat different individual from the one to be found in real life in the Southern states. But it was this

type of darky that the white minstrels strove
to imitate or, better stated perhaps, created and
perpetuated.[8]

Although Negroes sang in the streets of New
York, Philadelphia and other Eastern cities, probably to banjo accompaniment, as early as the American Revolution and were well established by the
early nineteenth century as popular city street entertainers, it is impossible to determine beyond dispute
when the first white actor did a blackface performance on the American stage, or who it was who presented the first Negro act in white theatres. As
early as 1769, during the presentation of Isaac Bick-
erstaff's comic opera, *The Padlock,* in New York,
Lewis Hallam, who was impersonating a Negro
slave, got drunk on the stage to the delight of his
audience. For 1795, there is a fragmentary record
which seems to establish the fact that the good people of Boston opposed a performance by a group of
Negro comedians who had come to the New England metropolis to entertain the natives. The next
year, however, a certain John Taylor sang a ballad
of slave life in Boston, perhaps in blackface.[9] In
1795, moreover, a genuine American Negro appeared on the stage of Philadelphia's Chestnut Street

[8] See Gaines, *op. cit.,* p. 17.
[9] *Ibid.,* p. 97.

Theatre in Murdock's *Triumphs of Love,* playing the part of Sambo.[10]

Just before the close of the eighteenth century, in 1799, Gottlieb Graupner sang "The Negro Boy," in Negro make-up, at the Federal Theatre in Boston, at the end of the second act of a play called *Oroonoko, or, the Royal Slave.* He won such applause that he had to bring in his little bench and sing his story over and over again.

This famous old theatre, planned by Charles Bulfinch, was located at the corner of Federal and Franklin Street, and had been opened five years previously. It was quite a pretentious structure, one hundred and forty feet long, sixty-two feet wide, and forty feet high. The building was of brick, with stone facings, iron posts and pillars, and projecting arcade in front, enabling carriages to land the company under cover. The audience passed through an elegant saloon to staircases leading to the rear of the boxes. "Guests" were met at the door by bewigged and bepowdered ushers, and conducted to their seats by candle light or whale-oil lamps, the only means of illumination. The interior of the theatre was circular, with an arched ceiling resting on Corinthian pillars. There were two rows of boxes, and separate side entrances to pit and gallery. Over the stage the coats of arms of the United

[10] Arthur Hobson Quinn, *A History of the American Drama* (New York, 1923), I, 332.

States and of the Commonwealth of Massachusetts had been painted. The walls were azure, the columns and fronts of the boxes straw and lilac color, the balustrades gilded, and the boxes hung with crimson silk. The building also included a dancing pavilion, card and tea rooms, and a kitchen. The magnificence of this early theatre, however, did not prevent the rowdies who frequented the galleries from pelting the musicians and sometimes other performers with apple cores and orange peelings.[11]

There is some question about the details of Graupner's appearance in this famous playhouse in Negro make-up. One version of the story adds the interesting detail that this pioneer minstrel sang his song to banjo accompaniment. That the performer was a skilled musician can be established beyond dispute. Whether he made his initial appearance during the particular season of the year when the theatre was in mourning because the news of President Washington's death had just reached the city, is more open to challenge. Besides the importance of this German immigrant in the history of blackface art, Graupner has still another claim to fame. Born in Hanover, Germany, he had served in a British regiment, and had come to Boston by way of Charleston, South 'Carolina. An excellent oboe player and an all-round musician, he organized, with

[11] Mary Caroline Crawford, *The Romance of the American Theatre* (Boston, 1913), pp. 114-115.

the support of the Russian consul, the first American orchestra consisting of himself and from ten to
twelve amateur performers who were living in Boston.  Graupner is known in musical history as "the
father of American orchestral music."  In 1809, we
find him again playing blackface parts with a circus
at Taunton, Massachusetts.[12]  For a considerable
period in the early nineteenth century Negro clowns
were extremely popular, and hardly a circus was
complete without a blackface performer.

In 1802, when summer gardens with fireworks
and summer theatricals were becoming popular in
New York City, a Mrs. Hodgkinson, in connection
with the play *A New Way to Win Hearts,* sang a
new song at the Mount Vernon Gardens, entitled
"Negro Philosophy" and it has been suggested that
her performance may belong to the preliminary
chapter on Negro minstrelsy.[13]  Sometime during
1814 or 1815, another performer, in the character
of a Negro sailor, sang "The Battle of Plattsburgh,"
a patriotic song about the War of 1812 in the Lake
Champlain region.  According to one account, the
singer was "Pig Pie" or "Pot Pie Herbert," an en-

[12] See Lawrence Hutton, "The Negro on the Stage," *Harper's
Magazine,* LXXIX, 133-134, and *Curiosities of the American Stage*
(New York, 1891), pp. 89-144; W. W. Clapp, Jr., *A Record of the
Boston Stage* (Boston, 1853) and Edward LeRoy Rice, *Monarchs of
Minstrelsy* (New York, 1911), p. 5.

[13] George C. D. Odell, *Annals of the New York Stage* (New York,
1927), II, 146.

terprising salesman of pies who promoted the sale of his wares by blackface advertising skits. Other versions of the story connect the performance with Sam Tatnall, who is said to have first used this darky jingle in 1814 while appearing with a circus in Albany, or with "Hop" Robinson (later spelled Robertson), who sang the song in New York during the intermission between a farce and the regular play.[14]

By far the most interesting contender for the honor of having been the first to sing this rather worthless patriotic jingle was Andrew Jackson ("Dummy") Allen. Perhaps because of Allen's exciting and fascinating career, his claim to priority has not lacked vigorous supporters. "Dummy" Allen was born in New York, during the last quarter of the eighteenth century. If we accept 1776, the earlier date generally given for his birth, it becomes possible to believe Allen's own account of his début as an actor in the rôle of page or incense boy in *Romeo and Juliet* (1786) and his claim, advanced in later years, that he was "The Father of the American Stage" and the oldest living actor. On the other hand, it must always be remembered that Allen had an inordinate fondness for associating the important dates in his own career with great events in the nation's history, and that in his eagerness for notoriety, he never displayed any particular attach-

---

[14] See Gaines, *op. cit.*, p. 97; Odell, *op. cit.*, II, 442; Rice, *op. cit.*, p. 5, and Hutton, *The Negro on the Stage*, p. 134.

ment for the truth.   Allen was extremely deaf, and
made a better servant and cook than an actor.   In
1829, he assumed the name of President Jackson,
after the latter's elevation to the presidency.

It was shortly after the news of Jackson's victory over the British in 1814 at New Orleans reached
the North that Allen played the part of a Negro in
*The Battle of Lake Champlain,* at the old Green
Street Theatre in Albany, New York.   It was in
this connection and sometime during 1815, that the
champions of the claims of this eccentric actor con-
tend Allen sang one of the earliest Negro songs ever
heard on the American stage.   Several stanzas have
been preserved, but the music seems to have been
lost.   "Dummy" Allen sang in Negro dialect

> Backside Albany, stan' Lake Champlain,
> Little pond, half full o' water;
> Platte-burg dar too, close 'pon de main;
> Town small, he grow big hereartèr.
>
> .   .   .   .   .
>
> On Lake Champlain, Uncle Sam set he boat,
> An Massa McDonough he sail 'em;
> While General Macomb make Platte-burg he home
> Wid de army whose courage nebber fail 'em.

Allen has other claims to fame.   For years he
served as the costumer and personal slave of the
great Edwin Forrest, and in 1817, he invented a
special kind of silver leather used by many actors
for their stage costumes.   At various stages in his

career Allen claimed to have managed theatres in Pensacola and Cincinnati. In 1816, when gas lighting was first made possible at the Chestnut Street Theatre in Philadelphia through the construction of expensive private gas works, Allen was a member of the company, playing inferior parts. Eight years later, he was employed as costumer and character actor at the Chatham Garden Theatre in New York —a huge and famous structure extending over several lots, with two circles of boxes, a large pit, and gaudy decorations of fawn-color, sky-blue, gilt, and crimson cushions. In 1826, Allen received a benefit at this theatre, and played Goldfinch in *The Road to Ruin,* and Francisco in *A Tale of Mystery.*[15]

Allen also operated restaurants in New York and Albany, and there is abundant evidence that he exercised his culinary gifts to the fullest satisfaction of his many patrons. There is a legend that his eating places were specially noted for their fine turtle soup, although very little turtle seems to have entered into the compound which Allen served his customers. Again and again, Allen yielded to the call of the stage. He appeared in various rôles in opera and drama, usually playing villain or clown parts, or rôles that enabled him to appear in his favorite equipment of slouched hat, broad buckles and sword at his side. His street attire of fuzzy white hat,

[15] See William B. Wood, *Personal Recollections of the Stage* (Philadelphia, 1855), p. 206; and Odell, *op. cit.,* III, 120, 207.

blue coat with huge brass buttons, and knotty cane, revealed the same eccentricities. At one time in his career when he was particularly pressed by his creditors, he arranged balloon ascensions in Ohio and Virginia. Allen died in New York, in 1853, while in the costume business. The grave of this eccentric Negro performer is marked by a monument bearing the grandiloquent inscription, "From his cradle he was a scholar; exceedingly wise, fair-spoken, and persuading; lofty and sour to them that loved him not but to those men that sought him sweet as summer."[16]

Many of the earliest blackface performers have left little record of their work. Comparatively little is known about such pioneers of minstrelsy as George Nichols, Bob Farrell (popularly known as "Zip Coon"), Bill Keller, Horatio Eversell, Barney Burns, John and Frank Whitaker, George Rice and William M. Hall. George Nichols, a clown in a circus, claimed to have been one of the first minstrels, and with Farrell disputed with George Washington Dixon the authorship of "Zip Coon," one of minstrelsy's earliest and most characteristic and popular

[16] For details of Allen's career see Lawrence Hutton, "The Negro on the Stage," *loc. cit.*, p. 135; T. Allston Brown, *History of the American Stage* (New York, 1870), I, 9; Sol Smith, *The Theatrical Journey—Work and Anecdotical Recollections of Sol Smith* (Philadelphia, 1854), pp. 221-229; H. P. Phelps, *Players of a Century: A Record of the Albany Stage* (Albany, 1880), p. 165; H. D. Stone, *Personal Recollections of the Drama* (Albany, 1873), pp. 173-180; Rice, *op. cit.*, p. 6.

songs. It resembled a rough jig dance, called "Natchez under the Hill," and was said to have originated among the boatmen, gamblers, river pirates and courtesans who congregated frequently for a real "hoe-down" at a rendezvous near Natchez. Nichols in all probability was the composer of "Roley Boley," sung by Lewis Hyell, and was the first to sing another early favorite, "Clare de Kitchen," at a public performance. The song he had adapted from a melody which he had heard sung by Negro firemen on the Mississippi River. James Roberts, in Negro character and wearing the uniform of a Continental soldier, sang the song, "Massa George Washington and Massa Lafayette," in October, 1824, at the Chatham Garden Theatre in New York City.

For years George Nichols was a clown for Purdy Brown's Theatre and Circus of the South and West. He had practically no formal education, but he could compose endless verses for comic songs, a feat which he often performed ten minutes before the time of his stage appearance. It has been claimed that Nichols sang "Jim Crow," the song "Daddy" Rice made famous, years before Rice made his début on the minstrel stage. Nichols had played clown parts, and is said to have sung the song first in white face, then in Negro make-up. The idea he got from a French darky banjo player, known throughout the

Mississippi Valley as Picayune Butler, a peripatetic performer who passed the hat and sang, "Picayune Butler is Going Away." Many of the airs used by this Negro minstrel were learned from another curious New Orleans darky, known as "Old Corn Meal." The latter made a living traveling over the countryside with a cart and horse, selling Indian meal. "Old Corn Meal" frequently sang his songs even at such fashionable places as the famous old Bishop's Hotel in New Orleans. He had, according to all accounts, a fine baritone voice, which he easily transformed into a ringing falsetto.[17]

George Washington Dixon, one of the best known of the early Negro impersonators, made his début in Albany, in 1827, while playing with a circus. The next year he appeared in the Chatham Theatre in New York City in what might be styled a Negro burlesque. He was among the first to sing the popular minstrel songs, "Coal Black Rose" and "Long Tailed Blue." During the fall of 1829, Chatham Theatre was occupied principally with the production of Dixon's Negro burlettas, in which the principal actor was supported by a rather "indifferent company."[18]

[17] See T. Allston Brown, "The Origin of Minstrelsy," in Charles H. Day, *Fun in Black* (New York, 1874).

[18] See Joseph N. Ireland, *Records of the New York Stage from 1750 to 1860* (New York, 1866), I, 585-586, 618, 633; and R. L. Wright, *Hawkers and Walkers* (Philadelphia, 1927), p. 188.

Dixon's increasing popularity in New York during the summer of 1829 was of great historical importance, for it indicated the growing interest of the public in Negro impersonations. On July 28, this "celebrated American Buffo Singer" was presenting "Analisation" and "The Coal Black Rose," in character, at the Bowery Theatre. In the fall, he introduced a new song, "The Lottery Ticket." He repeated these successes at the American Opera House and at the Park Theatre. At a special benefit for Dixon at the Chatham, in 1831, he sang all the old favorites, and introduced such new sensations as "Politicians look out, or Ladies make the best prime ministers, commanders, generals, lawyers, judges, doctors, distillers, upholsterers, and politicians"; "Love and Oysters"; "Major Longbow"; "March for Liberty and Glory, or Lafayette in France"; and "Firemen of the Nation," dedicated to the fire fighters of New York City.[19] Indeed it became the practice to put in these Negro character songs as features of almost any theatre program, whether devoted to farce comedy or heavy tragedy. Toward the close of his career this erstwhile minstrel star acquired much notoriety, first as a filibuster in Yucatan, and later as editor of a blackmailing scandal sheet in New York. Dixon died in the Charity Hospital in New Orleans, in 1861.[20]

[19] Odell, *op. cit.*, III, 468, 528, 354, 413, 421.
[20] Phelps, *op. cit.*, pp. 144, 165.

Thus there were many blackface performers in the United States before 1830, although the record of their activities is based on very fragmentary accounts which should be used with the greatest caution. Many actors blacked up for specific occasions, and appeared between acts in impersonations of plantation and steamboat darkies. Many Negro songs were sung by clowns from the backs of horses cantering around the sawdust ring of the circus. But although he had many predecessors, some of them of more than passing importance, the genuine minstrel performer, the first real prince of the burnt cork, was born when Thomas Dartmouth Rice began his impersonation of "Jim Crow."

To "Daddy" Rice or "Jim Crow" Rice, as he was often called, properly belongs the title of "father of American minstrelsy." It was Rice who gave the first entertainment in which a blackface performer was not only the main actor, but the entire act. Rice's impersonation of "Jim Crow," moreover, depended for its dramatic success entirely upon the performer's ability as an imitator of the voice, appearance and action of a genuine Negro character. Rice's mimicry was superb and absolutely true to life. His unexpected popularity as a Negro imitator brought him great financial returns and thus stimulated others to follow in his footsteps in an effort to duplicate his stage success. No less an artist than the great Joseph Jefferson called Rice "the first and best knight of the burnt-cork."

Thomas Dartmouth Rice has become almost a legendary figure in the history of minstrelsy. Consequently it is difficult to verify some of the details of his interesting career, although there is general agreement upon the essentials. The date of his first appearance in his famous "Jim Crow" rôle has been fixed anywhere between 1828 and 1831, and the reminiscences and memoirs of actors and theatrical managers of the period are particularly confusing on this point. Moreover, in strict accordance with the custom in the case of most legendary heroes, several cities are rivals for the honor of having been the first to witness the original "Jim Crow" performance.

Rice was born of poor parents in the old Seventh Ward of the city of New York, on May 20, 1808. As a youth, he learned the trade of wood carver. Occasionally, he served as a supernumerary at the Park Theatre. There is a tale to the effect that while serving as a "supe" at the Park Theatre, Rice attracted so much attention by his eccentricities in *Bombastes Furioso* that the leading characters in the play insisted upon his dismissal from the cast.[21] He soon abandoned his career as an artisan to take to the open road as an itinerant player.

[21] Odell, *op. cit.*, III, 632.

It was in a day when the lot of these itinerant Thespians, especially on the Ohio Valley frontier to which Rice's travels led him, was anything but a happy and pleasant one. Denounced by small-town preachers as agents of the devil, viewed by respectable citizens as troublesome vagrants, and occasionally arrested by the police as suspicious characters without visible means of support, these troubadours and minnesingers of America nevertheless sang and danced and played their way through the crude, raw, frontier settlements of Ohio, Kentucky, and Tennessee. In the earliest stages of these frontier theatricals, the strolling player recruited his supporting company from among the local amateurs, but traveling companies soon reduced the functions of these amateur actors to those of supernumeraries. Many performers met with bitter disappointment, but always "it was the call of the road, felt by actor and manager alike, and the ever-recurring hope that in the next town great fortunes awaited them which kept up their zest."[22] Even in the "triste little town of Cincinnati," already notable for its immigrant population, the theatre was poorly supported. Youthful patrons of public amusements preferred Dorfeuille's Hell with its chambers of horrors and electrical shocks, while the older members of the

[22] An interesting and valuable study is Helen Langworthy, *The Theatre in the Lower Valley of Ohio, 1797-1860*, an M.A. Thesis at the State University of Iowa, 1926.

community attended lectures on subjects like "The Fifth (or Gallinaceous) Order of Birds, after which the Nitrous Oxide will be administered."[23]

It was, in all probability, as one of these itinerant players that Rice reached the Ohio Valley states. For a time he was employed in Ludlow and Smith's Southern Theatre in Louisville, Kentucky, as property man, lamp lighter and stage carpenter. In 1828, Rice was a member of Samuel Drake's company at the Louisville Theatre, playing inferior stock parts. In this capacity, on one occasion he played the part of a Kentucky cornfield Negro in a local drama, Solon Robinson's *The Rifle*. It was as an interpolation between the acts of this play that Rice first sang and jumped "Jim Crow."

The details of this initial appearance vary somewhat, according to which account is followed, while Louisville, Cincinnati, and Pittsburgh have had their supporters on the question of where the act was first presented. Involved in this controversy of course is the question where Rice found the pattern or prototype for his "Jim Crow," and on this issue, Memphis and Nashville should be added to the list of cities already named, although there is little evidence to substantiate their claims to minstrel fame. Moreover, at about the time Rice was introducing his act, another darky, "Old Corn Meal," was being copied

[23] Gilbert Seldes, *The Stammering Century* (New York, 1928), pp. 42-43.

on the New Orleans stage.[24]   In spite of conflicting
testimony, however, there can be little disagreement
about the essentials of the "Jim Crow" story.

One day while Rice was walking through the
streets of one of these Middle Western towns, Louisville in all probability, or perhaps along its river
front, he encountered an old slave crooning an odd
melody and doing a curious shuffling step each time
he reached the chorus of his little song.   According
to one account, the Negro was cleaning and rubbing
down the horses in the stable-yard near the Louisville theatre where Rice was then playing.   The
original Jim Crow must have been a curious and interesting figure, a strange mixture of pathos and
humor.   His right shoulder was deformed and drawn
up high; his left leg was gnarled with rheumatism,
stiff and crooked at the knee, so that the Negro

[24] For various opinions on these disputed questions, see Arthur
Hornblow, *A History of the Theatre in America* (Philadelphia,
1919), II, 107 ff.; Walter M. Leman, *Memories of an Old Actor*
(San Francisco, 1886), p. 92; Rice, *op. cit.*, pp. 7-10; Brown, *History
of the American Stage*, p. 310; Quinn, *op. cit.*, p. 334; Phelps, *op. cit.*,
pp. 166-167; F. C. Wemyss, *Theatrical Biography of Eminent Actors
and Authors* (New York, 1852?), p. 122; Wemyss, *Theatrical Biography, or the Life of an Actor and Manager* (Glasgow, 1848), pp.
178-180; Stone, *op. cit.*, pp. 240-241; Sol Smith, *op. cit.*, p. 53; N. M.
Ludlow, *Dramatic Life as I Found It* (St. Louis, 1880), pp. 392-393;
M. B. Leavitt, *Fifty Years of Theatrical Management* (New York,
1912), p. 24; J. J. Jennings, *Theatrical and Circus Life* (St. Louis,
1882), p. 368; Marian Spitzer, "The Lay of the Last Minstrel," in
*The Saturday Evening Post*, March 7, 1925, pp. 12 ff.; and Dorothy
Anne Dondore, *The Prairie and the Making of Middle America*
(Cedar Rapids, 1928), p. 382.

walked with a limp, obviously painful and yet laughable. As he worked, he sang a rather mournful tune and, at the end of each stanza, gave a queer little jump, setting his "heel-a-rickin" as he alighted.

Rice was struck with the idea of imitating this curious figure on the stage. Such mimicry at least would furnish a pleasant variation from the stage Irishman with the shillalah, so popular in American playhouses at that time. Rice copied the walk and dress of his Negro model, memorized the stanzas of his curious song and improvised many others. Then he asked his manager for an opportunity to try his new act on the public. The "Jim Crow" song accordingly was interpolated in the local drama, and it proved to be popular immediately. Though its stanzas were senseless and their meter atrocious, the song was received by an outburst of applause and enthusiasm which must be accepted as a real tribute to Rice's unusual powers as a delineator of Negro character. The song and dance became a minstrel sensation.

The complete version of the song, together with the music, has been reprinted in Paskman and Spaeth's *Gentlemen, Be Seated*.[25] Only two stanzas need be quoted here, for many versions of the song still are afloat in all parts of the United States. Rice sang

[25] Pp. 12-14.

> I went down to creek, I went down a-fishing,
> I axed the old miller to gim me chaw tobacker
> To treat old Aunt Hanner.
>
> .   .   .   .   .
>
> I goes down to de branch to pester old miller,
> I wants a little light wood;
> I belongs to Capt. Hawkins and don't care a d—n.

Then after each stanza, the famous chorus,

> First on de heel tap, den on de toe,
> Ebery time I wheel about I jump Jim Crow.
> Wheel about and turn about and do jis so,
> And every time I wheel about I jump Jim Crow.

Rice next presented his new sketch at the Columbia Theatre in Cincinnati, interpolating the skit between acts. Then he tried his skill on a Pittsburgh audience. He appeared on the stage attired in the dilapidated coat, worn-out shoes and straw hat of a shiftless Negro. His success was even greater in Pennsylvania than it had been in Kentucky. Rice was tall and slender, a fact that added greatly to his success in his new Negro rôle, and he was one of the cleverest performers of all time in imitating the shambling gait and the plantation dialect of the American Negro. In Pittsburgh, Rice began improvising stanzas on local people and local situations, but the chorus of his "Jim Crow" song always remained the same. It was in this city also that he induced a friend, William C. Peters, to write out the music of his song, and soon copies of the new "song hit" were on sale throughout the United States. One writer on the history of the stage maintained that "Jim Crow" attained a popularity "unequalled by anything of the kind before or since."[26] Certainly it "wheeled about its lucky chanter from poverty to fame and fortune."

Rice next appeared as "Jim Crow" in the Walnut Street Theatre of Philadelphia, a large marble front summer theatre, and at the Warren Theatre in Boston. Late in 1832, "Jim Crow" Rice, as he was now known in the theatrical world, made his début at the Bowery Theatre in New York City, where he probably drew more money into the box office than any American performer in the same period of time. He was encored twenty times.

The song not only conquered America, but also became London's greatest song hit of the century. According to Bayard Taylor, the song was sung in Delhi by Hindu minstrels. In later years, and in a greatly modified form, it was reëchoed in Uncle Remus. The name "Jim Crow" legislation also probably has its origin in Daddy Rice's song.

On November 9, 1832, the New York press contained the sensational announcement that "Mr. Rice, whose celebrated song of 'Jim Crow' has drawn crowded houses in Baltimore, Philadelphia, etc. is daily expected. . . ." Rice "jumped" the first time

[26] Ireland, *op. cit.*, II, 55.

in New York three days later, inserting his specialty between two serious dramas, *The Hunchback* and *Catherine of Cleves,* and on the day following, between performances of *The Fire Raiser* and *The French Spy.* On November 15, he "jumped Jim Crow" at the Bowery, following a performance of *Othello.*[27] The audience "cried and laughed" as Rice jumped his "Jim Crow" between tragedy and farce at the Old Bowery, where he shared the stage with the great Booth, who was playing at the time in *The Apostate.*[28] In Washington, Rice varied his act by using the four year old Joseph Jefferson as a partner. Rice dressed up the lad to represent a miniature Jim Crow, blacked his face, put him in a large sack, and came to the footlights singing

Ladies and Gentlemen, I'd have you for to know
That I've got a little darkey here that jumps Jim Crow.

At this point in the song, the little blacked-up boy was dumped from the sack upon the stage. The incident seems to be well authenticated; but regardless of whether or not the great Jefferson actually made his first bow to the public in this fashion, it is established beyond dispute that in the early years of his theatrical career he imitated various Negro performers.

[27] Odell, *op. cit.,* III, 631.
[28] See Ireland, *op. cit.,* II, 55; and John B. Gough, *Sunlight and Shadows, or Gleanings from My Life Work* (Hartford, 1881), p. 527. See also N. I. White, "The White Man in the Woodpile," *American Speech,* IV, No. 3 (February 1929), pp. 209-210.

"Daddy" Rice's reputation was made. In 1836, he appeared in London, and became a sensation. Chimney sweeps and urchins imitated his gait as they roamed through the streets of the English metropolis. Rice sang many other Negro songs and also wrote numerous farces. One of his better known renditions contained the idiotic line, "Kitty-co-dink-a-ho-dink! oh, oh, roley-boley-Good morning, ladies all!" Rice was equally successful in the rôle of a plantation hand and in his portrayal of the "fancy Negro," or "dandy darky," whom he depicted in such numbers as "Dandy Jim of Caroline" and "Spruce Pink." In Dublin, Rice played to a house of eighteen hundred dollars, and in Cork he drew nineteen hundred dollars to the box office for one performance. His personal share on these tours was usually one-third of the receipts and, for a time, he commanded the highest salary of any minstrel performer.

Rice wrote a Negro extravaganza on the plot of *Othello*, collected many Negro melodies, and wove them into medleys like "Bone Squash" and "Virginny Cupids," or "The Virginny Mummy." Thus he became the creator of what was known for a time as "Ethiopian Opera." In these Negro "operas," Rice cleverly introduced old Negro songs into his own libretto. Some of his compositions were rather gross and vulgar in line and action, but this does not seem to have affected their success.

Many farces were born from Rice's fertile imagination. As early as January, 1833, he was introducing to Bowery Theatre audiences the new "Ethiopian Opera," called "Long Island Juba," or "Love by the Bushel," with a cast of four characters. In May of the same year, he produced "Where's My Head?" His creations included—"Bone Squash," "The Foreign Prince," "Jumbo Jum," "Black Pompey," "Wheugh! Here's a Go!," "The Sarcophagus," "The Black Cupid," "Uncle Pop," "Janggaroo," "The Hypocrite," "The Peacock and the Crow."

Little is known of these Ethiopian farces, but perhaps some notion of the kind of humor they represented may be derived from their *dramatis personae*. In one of the most famous, "Bone Squash Diavolo," the cast included Bone Squash, Paganini Brown, Spruce Pink, Pompey Ducklegs, Mose Sharpshins, Major Sam Switchell, Amos, Juanita Ducklegs, Tanza Snowball, and Jemima Flatheel. In another, "Black Hercules, or the Knave of Clubs," the characters were Sambo, Clever, Cornova, Bobby, and Lady Mullwood, while in "Wheugh! Here's a Go! or, City Portraits," appeared Sip Larkins, Old Traverson, Harry Markham, Fritz, the friseur, de Molge, Mrs. Trainer, and Melpomene. How far removed these creations were from any genuine Negro themes must be apparent. In the spring of 1840, when Rice returned from one of his frequent trips abroad, he opened at the Bowery Theatre with "Jim Crow in Foreign Service." Later he presented "Jim Crow in London," appearing as a "bootblack in extraordinary to the Court" while John Smith and Master Coleman danced "their original breakdown."[29]

There can be little doubt that these attempts at "Ethiopian Opera" by Rice were the precursors of the minstrel sketches that became an established feature of minstrel show programs in later years. The public of the 1840's never seemed to tire of these nonsensical performances. One New York editor described his emotions while witnessing a Rice performance during the summer of 1840 in the following terms: "Entering the theatre, we found it crammed from pit to dome, and the best representative of our American Negro that we ever saw was stretching every mouth in the house to its utmost tension. Such a natural gait!—such a laugh!—and such a twitching-up of the arm and shoulder! It was *the* Negro, par excellence. Long live James Crow, Esquire!"[30]

Strangely enough, Rice played in very few minstrel shows. He preferred to act alone, or to perform between the acts of a more serious play. Charley White's Serenaders and Wood's Minstrels

[29] Odell, *op. cit.*, III, 635, 686; IV, 73, 636, 481, 484, 372.
[30] Quoted in Odell, *op. cit.*, IV, 372.

were among the few minstrel companies that could enlist the services of this "father of minstrelsy." His last engagement was with the latter company, in 1858. For two decades Rice was almost constantly before the public. In 1847, he returned to the Chatham Theatre in the rôles of "Jumbo Jum" and "Ginger Blue"; and in 1851, he staged a revival of "Jim Crow" at the National Theatre in New York. On this occasion, however, he discovered rather quickly that his earlier drawing power at the box office no longer existed. Toward the close of his career, Rice also played the rôle of Uncle Tom in the great anti-slavery propaganda drama which was sweeping the North in the 'fifties. He also appeared in Cincinnati in plays like *Paul Pry* and *Guy Mannering*.[31]

Ten years before his death, "Daddy" Rice was stricken with paralysis which temporarily deprived him of the use of his limbs. Although he recovered from this stroke, he was left with greatly impaired health. His eccentricities increased after this misfortune, particularly his habit of using five and ten dollar coins for buttons on his coat and vest. In September, 1860, when he suffered a second stroke of paralysis, Rice was in real financial distress. He had squandered his fortune in careless if not riotous

[31] See Langworthy, *op. cit.*, Appendix D.

living, and the father of minstrelsy died practically
without a home or a friend.[32]

Rice had many imitators who were eager to reap
the popularity and the financial rewards that this
new form of entertainment seemed to hold out to
the ambitious and clever actor. In 1830, Bill Keller,
a former "low comedian," was singing "Coal Black
Rose" very successfully. Almost simultaneously,
Barney Burns, a job actor of little reputation, made
popular such minstrel songs as "My Long Tail
Blue" and "Such a Getting Up Stairs," composed
by Joe Blackburne.[33] Graham and Blakely were
singing "Jim Crow" at two theatres in New York
during the 1833 season, and McQuire and Graham
presented "The Ethiopian Rivals, or Jim and Jack
Crow," during the same season, in response to the
Rice craze.[34] Bob Farrell sang "Zip Coon" at the
Bowery in 1834;[35] and in 1835, Miss Wray, "the
young American phenomenon" who was but seven
years old, was brought from a circus at Richmond-
Hill to the Olympic Pavilion in New York to do her
Jim Crow specialty.[36] In 1833, Thomas H. Blakely,
a fairly well known actor, sang a "Comic Extrav-

[32] For other interesting details about Rice, see Rice, *op. cit.*, pp.
7-11; Leavitt, *op. cit.*, p. 24; Leman, *op. cit.*, p. 92; Ludlow, *op. cit.*,
p. 392; Wemyss, *Twenty-Six Years of the Life of an Actor and
Manager* (New York, 1847), I, 206.

[33] Jennings, *op. cit.*, p. 368.

[34] Odell, *op. cit.*, III, 646.

[35] *Ibid.*, IV, 25.

[36] *Ibid.*, p. 43.

aganza of Jim Crow" in the intermission between two plays;[37] and in 1837, the brother of the original Rice "jumped Jim Crow" at the Franklin and Bowery Theatre in New York while his more famous brother was at the National.[38]　Late in the same decade, Barney Williams became famous for his Negro dances; and the enterprising P. T. Barnum featured Jack Diamond, one of the great dancers of all time, in an Ethiopian "break-down."　In October, 1837, a certain J. Henry was at the American Museum, exhibiting "the Ethiopian Comic Statues, or Sambo on the Pedestal."[39]　In 1841, several performers did Negro songs and dances at the Chatham Theatre, and returned a year later with new recruits added to their act.[40]　Thus, for a full decade before the first minstrel show was presented, individual actors blacked up and staged their specialties, either as single acts or during the intermission between acts of a regular play, and "Negro specialists" everywhere were much in demand.

Not only on the stage, but in the sawdust ring of the circus, Rice had many imitators.　It was not until the season of 1842-1843 in New York that the circus at last succeeded in separating itself from the theatre and in becoming a distinctive amusement in-

[37] Hutton, "The Negro on the Stage," *loc. cit.*, pp. 139-140.
[38] Ireland, *op. cit.*, I, 249, and Odell, *op. cit.*, IV, 239.
[39] Odell, *op. cit.*, IV, 256.
[40] See Gaines, *op. cit.*, p. 99; and Al G. Field, "History of American Minstrelsy," *The Kit Kat* (Columbus, O.), VIII, No. 2.

stitution.[41]   Even then equestrian drama frequently
was presented in the regular theatres.   It is not sur-
prising therefore that the early circus, which was .
hardly more than a variety bill to provide a whole
evening's entertainment, should have attached this
new and popular "Ethiopian drama" to its list of
other specialties.   Many of the early minstrel men
began their professional careers in the circus ring
and Negro acts in the days of Rice's amazing popularity were indispensable parts of almost every
circus.

In the season of 1839, Sanford, an early minstrel star, was singing "Jim Along Josey" in the
Broadway Theatre.[42]   At a circus in the Bowery
Amphitheatre, "Jim Crow's Visit," in which "all the
talented Ethiopians will appear," was conspicuously
advertised[43] in 1840.   During this season Master
John Diamond, the sensational dancer of "break-
downs," and "Massa" Pelham, one of the original
"Big Four" who organized the first minstrel com-
pany in America, also appeared with the same circus.
The former was famous in the sawdust ring long be-
fore he appeared as an Ethiopian dancer in the New
York theatres.   In Brooklyn, in 1843, Rockwell's
Equestrian Troupe advertised as a special feature

[41] For the early circus see I. J. Greenwood, *The Circus: Its Origin
and Growth Prior to 1835* (New York, 1898).
[42] Odell, *op. cit.*, IV, 420.
[43] *Ibid.*, p. 422.

of its circus performance, "the inimitable musical comicalities of the far famed *African Minstrels,* with their unique and truly melodious accompaniment of *Plantation Instruments,*" and it is significant that the circus stressed this minstrel feature as the main attraction of the bill.[44] During the same season, Welch's Olympic Circus presented Master Diamond in "Negro Doings," and interspersed Ethiopian concerts between various equestrian acts. These concerts were given by Whitlock, Brower, Pelham, and Emmett, the founders of the Virginia Minstrels. On one occasion, when these actors had a special benefit, three of them presented "Dan Tucker on Horseback."[45] Two years earlier, Whitlock had appeared in a song and banjo feature with the circus playing at the Arcadian Garden in New York and together with T. G. Booth and Diamond had presented Ethiopian trios. Another circus bill for the same season advertised "Virginny Melodies and Breakdowns."[46] At Barnum's Museum, Negro minstrelsy invaded the famous "lecture" room in 1842 and 1843, when Diamond and Whitlock, "Negro specialists"; the "Ethiopian Serenaders" or "Boston Minstrels," "six performers, each one of whom is a Professor of Music"; "George Western, denominated the Great Western, in Negro delin-

[44] Odell, *op. cit.,* IV, 697.
[45] *Ibid.,* p. 615.
[46] *Ibid.,* p. 589.

eations, imitations of an engine at full speed, etc.",
and Frank Brower performed.[47]

In the circus ring, in the regular theatres, and
in other places of amusement where Negro specialties were featured on almost every playbill, the minstrel show was struggling to be born. Blakely sang
"The Coal Black Rose" at Niblo's in 1840 for over
a hundred consecutive nights. Sanford was the
Ethiopian specialist at the Vauxhall Garden in New
York, together with Whitlock, "the King of Banjo
players and the Emperor of Extravaganza Singers,"
and Master Garrett "in the old Virginny break-
down."[48] At the old Bowery in 1841, Negro farces
like "Jim Along Josey," and "The Black Ghost, or
the Nigger turned Physician," served as afterpieces
to practically every legitimate drama.[49] At the
Franklin Theatre, "J. Morris' Concert and Olio
Company of more than Twenty Ladies and Gentlemen, with an admission fee of 12½ cents to all
parts of the theatre," presented programs featuring
gymnasts and contortionists; musical and dancing
numbers; and Negro acts by Pelham, "Backus, the
great Paganinny"; Dan Emmett, "the great Southern banjo melodist"; Frank Brower, "the perfect
representative of the Southern Negro Character";
and Master Pierce, "the great Heelologist." No

[47] Odell, *op. cit.*, IV, 666, 669.
[48] *Ibid.*, pp. 430, 434.
[49] *Ibid.*, p. 478.

gentleman was admitted to the first tier of boxes "at any price unless accompanied with a lady."[50] At the Chatham, Negro farces and other "ethiopian delights" were very popular.[51]

In January, 1843, the Amphitheatre of the Republic announced Billy Whitlock and Dan Gardner "in their original Serenade," and "Jim Crow, Esq. On Horseback," with R. W. Pelham as the Negro clown. Emmett and Brown meantime were presenting "Negro Holiday Sports in Carolina and Virginia" at a circus, while George Washington Dixon, "the Pedestrian and Melodist," and many other Negro character actors, were playing in other New York amusement centers.[52]

Most of the earliest blackface performers have long been forgotten. All of them performed as individual actors, and their impersonations of the life of the Negro on the Southern plantation not only were clever, but occasionally very true to life. But there were some indications also that the real darky was being transformed into the "joke-book" edition of the Negro for the stage, although this transformation was comparatively slow until minstrel shows as such began to develop. It is a notable fact that the first minstrel show, in which a troupe of burnt cork performers monopolized the whole per-

[50] Odell, *op. cit.*, IV, 664.
[51] *Ibid.*, p. 638.
[52] *Ibid.*, p. 674.

formance and thereby constructed an entirely new and distinctively American form of entertainment, did not come into existence until nearly a dozen years after "Daddy" Rice had made his sudden and phenomenal success as the impersonator of Jim Crow. But the birth of American minstrelsy might have been predicted for years before the famous "Virginia Minstrels" made their début. All the performers in this company had had theatrical or circus experience, and had presented various Negro and musical specialties. All that was necessary to produce a minstrel show was an arrangement of these various specialties into a coördinated program to fill an entire evening's performance.

Before proceeding to a discussion of the origin of minstrel shows in some detail, a word of caution may not be inappropriate here. Although the minstrels found the inspiration for their new art in the life of the Southern darky and occasionally presented accurate delineations of the types they were trying to imitate, it would be an error to assume that the minstrel performers, as a class, really consistently expressed Negro life and feeling in their theatrical performances. It must be admitted at once, and succeeding chapters will make this more evident, that many of the famous minstrel men were Northern-born-and-reared, or foreign-born immigrant white men, who had almost no first-hand knowledge of the Negro's manner of life. The subjects and ideas of many minstrel shows, in their later development at least, were Caucasian, and not Negro. Moreover, most of the great minstrel songs of the decade when minstrelsy was the leading form of theatrical entertainment, were written by white men, and only some of the earlier of these "Negro" songs had any original Negro basis. Many showed a closer relationship to other songs current in the 1810's and 1820's sung by early non-Negro "songsters," than to Negro folk music. The earlier minstrel melodies quickly established a conventional "Negro" song, which other minstrel composers were quick to imitate. If recent investigations have shown a correspondence between the old minstrel songs and melodies sung today by Negroes, the relationship may not be due to a survival of pre-minstrel, Negro folk music, but rather to Caucasian influence on the Negro.[53]

[53] See N. I. White, "The White Man in the Woodpile," in *American Speech*, Vol. IV, No. 3, February, 1929, p. 210; and his scholarly *American Negro Folk-Songs*.

# CHAPTER II

## EARLY MINSTREL SHOWS

The minstrel show, as has been said, was a natural and almost inevitable development from the performances of individual actors who had presented such popular skits and songs as "Jim Crow," "Clare de Kitchen," "Lucy Long," and other favorites. The popularity of these presentations had been little short of phenomenal. Negro acts were established features in menageries, museums, circuses, and theatres. Add the banjo, the fiddle, and a few players who could perform singly, in duets, trios, and quartettes; interject a few conundrums and darky puns and jokes; and close with a "hoe-down" dance in which every member could become as hilarious as he pleased, and the American minstrel show would be complete.

Probably the first public presentation of what may be called a real minstrel show took place in the Bowery Amphitheatre in New York City, early in 1843. There is still some controversy as to the exact time and place. Indeed, Christy's Minstrels dispute with the Virginia Minstrels the honor of having staged the first performance in America by a minstrel company, although the latter are given this distinction in most of the accounts that are available for this notable event in American theatrical history.

Minstrelsy was born in a decade when the fashionable American public had not yet become addicted to the theatre-going habit, and when the average American preferred to attend lectures on such subjects as mesmerism, animal magnetism, phrenology, and the new phenomenon of the electric telegraph. Religious revivals were flourishing, and the public was devoted to circuses, pantomimes, gorgeous displays of fireworks, and museums of natural wonders. In 1839, eight thousand people visited Dunn's Chinese Museum in Philadelphia during one week. The theatre therefore had to disguise its offerings under such euphonious announcements as "Moral, Instructive, Recreative and Temperate Amusements."[1]

The Virginia Minstrels were organized in New York City at the boarding house of a Mrs. Brooks on Catherine Street, where Daniel Decatur Emmett, one of the earliest and greatest of a long line of minstrel stars, happened to be living. The company consisted of four members, a quartette of friends, Emmett, Frank Brower, "Billy" Whitlock and "Dick" Pelham. Whitlock was a typesetter of the *New York Herald* by vocation, but his avocation was comedy and the banjo, and he excelled in both of these important departments of minstrelsy. Emmett, who was a fairly competent musician also, already had made various public appearances, includ-

[1] Meade Minnigerode, *The Fabulous Forties* (New York, 1924), pp. 149-150.

ing an engagement with a circus in Charleston, South Carolina, in 1841. All had had theatrical experience.

According to the generally accepted account, Whitlock, on one occasion, happened to be practicing on the banjo with his friend Emmett, when Brower and Pelham, quite by chance, came to call at Emmett's boarding house. It occurred to one of the group to develop an ensemble performance, with the result that the quartette began to practice for a public presentation of their minstrel acts. Emmett played the violin, Whitlock the banjo, Brower the bone castanets, and Pelham the tambourine. Their first show was presented either in Bartlett's billiard parlor in the Bowery, or in the Branch Hotel, a favorite rendezvous for showmen in New York City. Some of the leading circus men of that day, including Nathan Howes, were present to witness this first minstrel performance.

According to Emmett's account, many in the audience were disposed to ridicule the new experiment in theatricals, and the show began with the crowd jeering this new and strange musical combination of violin, banjo, bones and tambourine. For although the single blackface performer had become an established feature, this new combination had never been tried, not even on the comic stage. The costumes and other novel features of the program apparently were planned by Emmett. The performers were attired in white trousers, striped calico shirts, and blue calico coats made in dress suit style with long swallow-tails. The audience, in spite of the unfavorable beginning, became more attentive and interested as the show progressed. According to Emmett's account, "Brower's funny song made them howl with delight," Whitlock's songs were well received, and by the time Emmett sang, the little room was rocked by an "uproar of applause." It was in this unpretentious fashion that a distinctively American institution had its origin.

There is some conflicting evidence as to whether this initial production occurred in December, 1842, or early in 1843, although the latter date seems to be more generally accepted.[2] In February, 1843, probably on the sixth, these pioneers of minstrelsy ventured upon a public stage. Under the name of the Virginia Minstrels (sometimes also called the Virginia Serenaders) Emmett's minstrel quartette made their bow to the public in a benefit for Dick Pelham, a procedure that was very popular at the time as a device to increase box office receipts for the entire company. According to some accounts, the performance was given first at the Chatham Theatre; but if this was the case, the company soon

[2] Jennings, *op. cit.*, p. 367; and Hutton, "The Negro on the Stage," p. 141,

moved to the Bowery theatre. "The house was crowded and jammed with our friends," reported Whitlock, and his friend who was the beneficiary of this performance "of course put ducats in his purse." From all accounts, there was great interest in "the first night of the novel, grotesque, original and surpassingly melodious Ethiopian Band, entitled, the Virginia Minstrels," as the first show was eloquently described in language which became a feature of the extravagant advertisements and press stories of later minstrel performances. The announcement in the *New York Herald* characterized the show as "an exclusively minstrel entertainment combining the banjo, violin, bone castanets and the tambourine, and entirely exempt from the vulgarities and other objectionable features which have hitherto characterized Negro extravaganzas."[3] In the course of the evening's program, all four performers sang and danced, jigged in solo and double numbers, played their respective instruments singly and in various combinations, and did the "Lucy Long Walk Around" and "The Essence of Old Virginny," a dance and "break-down," at the close of the show. The last feature became established quite early in the history of minstrelsy as the traditional ending of the show's "first part." In describing the com-

[3] Rice, *op. cit.*, p. 11, and Odell, *op. cit.*, IV, 675.

pany, Emmett wrote, "We were all endmen and interlocutors."[4]

The Virginia Minstrels had a benefit on February 9 at the Amphitheatre and later appeared at the Park Theatre with Welch's Olympic Circus. They then ventured out into the provinces and began a tour of other leading cities. They were well received in Boston, at the Tremont Theatre, in March, 1843,[5] a theatre described by the visiting actor, Tyrone Power, as having "the most elegant exterior in the country."[6]

They returned to New York, and in April, 1843, left for performances in England. Although they played with some success in Liverpool, Manchester, and London, they were disappointed by their reception in the British Isles. Despite the fact that minstrelsy later became very popular in England, the Virginia Minstrels seemed to arouse little interest. Virtually stranded in a foreign country, the troupe disbanded and its members returned to America. Here they found employment in various minstrel companies which had sprung into existence during their absence abroad in an attempt to duplicate the

[4] For pictures of this first minstrel troupe, see Paskman and Spaeth, *op. cit.*, pp. 15, 19; and C. B. Galbreath, *Daniel Decatur Emmett* (Columbus, Ohio, 1904), p. 11.

[5] Leavitt, *op. cit.*, p. 23.

[6] Crawford, *op. cit.*, p. 253.

great success won by the Virginia Minstrels in their American appearance.[7]

Thus far the account deviates little from the generally accepted version, for indeed the story of Emmett's Virginia Minstrels almost has become one of the legends of minstrelsy. But even a casual and by no means exhaustive examination of the history of the American stage reveals the fact that there were other companies which may have antedated the Virginia Minstrels. As has been pointed out, in 1841 for example, a certain John Smith and "Mister" Coleman did Negro songs and dances at the Chatham Theatre; the next year they added two other members to their act, although it is doubtful whether their performance was more than one act in a larger production.[8] According to a letter written thirty years after the date usually given for the first minstrel show, by S. S. Sanford, himself a prominent minstrel performer, the birthplace of the Negro minstrel show was the Park Theatre, in New York, in 1841 or 1842, the company consisting of the same personnel as the Virginia Minstrels, except that Joe Sweeney played the violin instead of Dan Emmett. The Park Theatre at that time was "as well ap-

---

[7] For additional data on this first troupe, see Brander Matthews, "The Rise and Fall of Negro Minstrelsy," pp. 754-759; Brown, *History of the American Stage,* p. 413; Hutton, *Curiosities of the American Stage,* pp. 124, 126; and Gaines, *op. cit.,* p. 100.

[8] Gaines, *op. cit.,* p. 99.

pointed as any theatre out of London,"[9] horseshoe in form, with three tiers of boxes. From New York the company proceeded to Boston, "the maiden city where minstrelsy gave an entire evening's performance," according to Sanford, and thence the performers traveled to Europe.[10] Immediately after their departure, Sanford's account continues, numerous minstrel companies entered the theatrical field in the United States. Sanford himself played in a company organized by Hugh Lindsay, which included Dan Rice, Dan Minich, Tom Young, Master Roston and C. Von Bonhorst. Thereupon Sanford organized his own company in Philadelphia and played at Palmo's Concert Hall, the Chatham Theatre and the Pantheon in New York, and the Elysian Fields in Hoboken.

According to other accounts, the first company was composed, in 1843, of Whitlock, T. G. Booth, H. Mestayer and Barney Williams. Another version gives Frank Brower credit for organizing the first troupe in 1843, and some evidence can be adduced to show that the Christy company was formed as early as 1842, although it did not reach New York before 1846.[11] Probably the second troupe organized in New York was the Kentucky Minstrels, a company of five including Frank Lynch, T. G. Booth, Young

[9] Crawford, *op. cit.*, p. 251.
[10] See letter in *The New York Clipper*, May 28, 1871.
[11] Gaines, *op. cit.*, pp. 99 ff.

Richardson, and H. Mestayer. It is certain that
the Virginia, the Columbia, and the Kentucky Minstrels all played at the Chatham Theatre in 1843, the
Columbia Minstrels playing "to an audience that
had just been charmed by the Virginia Minstrels."[12]
Then followed the Ring and Parker Minstrels and
the Congo Melodists, although second place is sometimes given to the famous Christy Minstrels, while
evidence may be found to show that the last named
organization actually antedated the Virginia Minstrels by one year. Much of the proof for these
claims must rest entirely on reminiscences and theatrical memoirs, which are notably untrustworthy
sources of historical information.[13]

The original Christy Minstrels were organized
by E. P. Christy in Buffalo. Dan Emmett, in 1877,
in an effort to refute the claim that this was the
original troupe, argued that Enom Dickinson, who
had had experience in other companies, trained the
Christys in Buffalo while Emmett's band was touring England.[14] That Dickinson was associated with
the Christy organization in 1843 seems to be fairly
well established.[15] "Ned" Christy was a banjo and

[12] Odell, *op. cit.*, IV, 644.
[13] See also, Quinn, *op. cit.*, p. 334; and Ruth C. Dimmick, *Our
Theatres Today and Yesterday* (New York, 1913), pp. 82-83, and *The
New York Clipper*, February 21, 1857.
[14] Hutton, *Curiosities of the American Stage*, p. 132.
[15] T. Allston Brown, *History of the New York Stage, from the
First Performance in 1732 to 1901*, 3 vols. (New York, 1870), I, 364.

tambourine performer in the bar rooms and hotels frequented by the sailors and townsmen of Buffalo.[16] He made his début as a minstrel, with a banjo and a seedy wardrobe, at Harry Meech's Museum in Buffalo, and thus ventured upon the career that was destined to bring him fame in the city where everyone knew him and his antecedents.[17] His original troupe consisted of George N. Christy (whose real name was Harrington), L. Durand, and T. Vaughn. At first the company was known as The Virginia Minstrels, but this was changed to The Christy Minstrels, when Enom Dickinson, Zeke Bachus and Earl Pierce were added to the group.[18] From Buffalo the company seems to have gone to Milwaukee, and then to New York. The company opened at Palmo's Opera House, and on a second visit, performed at the Society Library Rooms, later known as Appleton's Building. Thence they moved to the Alhambra, near Prince Street, and then, in 1847, leased Mechanics Hall on Broadway. An advertisement announced

[16] See Nichols, *Forty Years of American Life* (L. John Maxwell, 1864), I, 134.

[17] Wright, *Hawkers and Walkers* (Philadelphia, 1927), p. 188; Stone, *op. cit.*, p. 241; Hornblow, *op. cit.*, II, 108; M. Minnigerode, *op. cit.*, pp. 230-232; Brown, *op. cit.*, I, 364.

[18] Jennings, *op. cit.*, p. 369; and *The New York Clipper*, February 21, 1857.

*Christy's*
far famed and original band of
*Ethiopian Minstrels*
whose unique and chaste performances have been
patronized by the elite and fashion in all the principal cities of the Union . . . respectfully announce
that they will give a series of their popular and inimitable concerts, introducing a variety of entirely new
songs, choruses and burlesques.
Admission, 25c[19]

Although some little time was required for the
public "to tutor themselves in Negro minstrelsy,"
as the first receipts of the show indicate,[20] the
Christy Minstrels became very popular and their
theatre was crowded nightly for years. They played
in Mechanics Hall for nine years and eleven months,
and E. P. Christy was for years the unchallenged
leader of his profession. In 1854, he was able to
retire from business with a considerable fortune.
Having invaded the theatrical metropolis in 1846
for a series of "concerts," the company remained for
almost a decade, playing continuously.[21] George
Christy also became wealthy from the enterprise and
after E. P. Christy's retirement, took over the show
and in association with Henry Wood, managed two
minstrel houses in New York, Mechanics' Hall and
Mitchell's Olympic.[22]

[19] Reprinted in Minnigerode, *op. cit.*, pp. 230-231.
[20] Davidge, *Footlight Flashes* (New York, 1866), p. 127.
[21] Minnigerode, *op. cit.*, pp. 230-231.
[22] Hutton, "The Negro on the Stage," p. 687.

George Christy's salary for two and a half years was reported to have reached the startling total of $19,680. The receipts of the show, which had yielded a profit of only three hundred dollars during the first year's run in New York, mounted rapidly. In 2,792 performances, the receipts were $317,-589.30, with profits of over $160,000 for the producers, although this was at a time when the admission charge was only twenty-five cents.[23] As a matter of fact, minstrel performances were beginning to attract the patronage of the most respectable citizens. Lyman Abbott, for example, relates in his *Reminiscences* that his father attended the Christy Minstrels regularly, because he found the singing excellent although the jokes often were bad.[24]

The Christy Minstrels gave the minstrel show the stereotyped form which it kept to the present time, with its semi-circular arrangement of the performers in the "first part," the interlocutor in the center and the endmen with bones and tambourines at the extremes, and with the highly colored suits, street parades and the variety acts of the olio, or "second part." E. P. Christy, the founder of the original "Christys," died in 1862, as the result of jumping from a second story window.

Almost every minstrel company of any importance toured England during the middle years of the

[23] See Jennings, *op. cit.*, p. 369.
[24] Quoted in M. R. Werner, *Barnum* (New York, 1926), p. 139.

last century. Here minstrelsy became extremely popular with all classes of the population. Even the learned Gladstone found relief from the cares of state among the sweet singers of minstrelsy and the comedy of the endmen, and attended minstrel shows regularly. For a time, the English called all Ethiopian performers "Christys" or "Christy Minstrels," "as they call all top-boots 'Wellingtons' and all policemen 'Bobbies.' "[25]

In May, 1871, the Royal Christy Minstrels were playing in Ross, England, the Queen's Christy Minstrels in Hereford, and Mathews' C. C. C. Christy Minstrels in Glasgow.[26] Many English cockneys tried to imitate the success of their American cousins by blacking up and presenting minstrel acts in Paris cafés and elsewhere on the Continent, though the "corner-men," as the English renamed the "endmen," had never seen a cotton field and must have learned their Negro dialect at least second or third hand

[25] Hutton, *Curiosities of the American Stage,* p. 132. Thackeray wrote on one occasion, "I heard a humorous balladist not long ago, a minstrel with wool on his head and an ultra-Ethiopian complexion, who performed a negro ballad that I confess moistened these spectacles in a most unexpected manner. I have gazed at thousands of tragedy queens dying on the stage, and expiring in appropriate blank verse, and I never wanted to wipe them. They have looked up, be it said, at many scores of clergymen without being dimmed, and behold! a vagabond with a corked face and a banjo sings a little song, strikes a wild note, which sets the heart thrilling with happy pity." Quoted by Brander Matthews, "The Rise and Fall of Negro Minstrelsy," p. 759.

[26] *The New York Clipper,* May 27, 1871.

from American actors.[27]  *The New York Clipper*
for December 11, 1858, carried a cut of The Court-
Costume Minstrel Band, a company of Ethiopian
delineators recently organized in London, and appearing in court costume with phenomenal success
before their British audiences.  *The London Illustrated News,* in a rather labored article, sought to
explain the extraordinary vogue of Negro minstrelsy in the British Isles, stating that "Nothing can
be more silly and absurd than these Negro rhymes,
the imperfections of which reckon among their attractions, a false rhyme taking the rank of a positive
beauty.  Yet out of all this nonsense, modulated as
it is by the cunning of these minstrels' art, there
somehow rises a humanizing influence which gives
to an innocent recreation a positive philanthropic
sentiment.  This sentiment connects itself with them
as a colored troupe.  With white faces the whole
affair would be intolerable.  It is the ebony that gives
the due and needful color to the monstrosities, the
breaches of decorum, the exaggerations of feeling,
and the 'silly, sooth' character of the whole implied
drama. . . ."

It is possible to note only a few of the pioneer
minstrel companies; for after the phenomenal success of these early ventures, minstrelsy rapidly became one of the most common and financially suc-

[27] *The Saturday Review* (London), LVII, 739.

cessful forms of American entertainment. "Charley" White, an accordeon player, organized The Kitchen Minstrels in 1844, on the second floor of a New York rooming house, and two years later, opened The Melodeon at 53 Broadway with his own troupe. One of the first companies in Pittsburgh was headed by Nelson Kneass, a singer, banjo player and pianist in the early 'forties.[28] The Pantheon was opened as a minstrel house in New York about 1846.[29] A year or two earlier, The Ethiopian Serenaders, consisting of Frank Germon, Stanwood, Winnemore, Quinn and others, had opened their show at Palmo's Opera House in New York, preparatory to a successful invasion of Europe where they played "three-a-day" for a time in England.[30] In 1846, when the company went to England, it included Germon, Stanwood, G. Warrington, G. Pelham, W. White and "Old Scotchy" Dumbolton. The invasion of the British Isles turned out to be a theatrical triumph. The company played morning and evening daily at the St. James Theatre in London for six weeks, and also performed by invitation at the homes of the nobility and before Queen Victoria at Arundel Castle. The latter is said to have presented each member of

[28] Robert P. Nevin, "Stephen C. Foster and Negro Minstrelsy," *Atlantic Monthly*, XX, 608-616.
[29] Brown, *History of the New York Stage*, I, 361.
[30] *Ibid.*, p. 339; Ruth C. Dimmick, *op. cit.*, pp. 83-93; Werner, *op. cit.*, p. 97; and *The New York Clipper*, February 21, 1857.

the company with a ring—at any rate, the story was useful to the press agent.

The Pantheon in New York also was the scene of Sam S. Sanford's first ventures into the minstrel field. There followed The Virginia Serenaders, organized in Philadelphia and including Cool White, James Sanford, Richard Myers and Robert Edwards. It was Sanford who introduced the popular song, "Carry Me Back to Old Virginny."[31] The Original Campbell Minstrels of John Campbell (a former restaurant keeper) became so popular that before the close of the 1850's, scores of other companies borrowed the name. The country was full of "Campbell's Minstrels," and occasionally two rival companies with identical names would meet on the same train with results that can readily be imagined. As early as 1843, the famous Buckley family, consisting of James Buckley and his three sons, R. Bishop, G. Swayne, and Fred, had entered the minstrel business, finally taking the name of Buckley's New Orleans Serenaders. This company performed in Boston for two years, and then toured the United States and England with great success. In 1852, the enterprising troupe visited California and played to large audiences in the gold-mining camps in tents at three dollars admission. The Buckley Serenaders probably were the first to produce burlesque opera as part of the regular program. One member of the

[31] Wright, *op. cit.*, p. 188.

family was a virtuoso on the Chinese fiddle. Another was skillful with the bones and imitated drums, marching soldiers and horse-racing with great success. Later, he appeared in an act called "Musical Moments," playing no less than twelve instruments.[32]

The Sable Brothers, Harmoneons, White's Serenaders, Nightingale Serenaders, Sanford's Opera Troupe, Slighter's Empire Minstrels, Fellow's Minstrels, Washington Utopians, Ordway's Aeolians, Pierce's Minstrels, Horn and White's Opera Troupe, Norris Campbell's Minstrels, and the Sable Harmonists,—these and many other minstrel companies with equally fantastic names were in the heyday of their success in the middle of the nineteenth century.[33]

[32] Rice, *op. cit.*, pp. 15 ff.; Minnigerode, *op. cit.*, p. 232.

[33] Dimmick, *op. cit.*, pp. 82-83. Other notable companies of a somewhat later period included, Whitmore and Clarke's; Delehanty, Hengler, Horn and Bloodgood's; Dougherty, Mack, Barney and Wild's; Cotton and Murphy's; and Hooley's Megatherians. See Barney Fagan, "Minstrels," in *Stage and Foyer,* March, 1926, pp. 41-42. *The New York Clipper,* April 23, 1859, lists, in the order of their origin, the leading companies in existence at the close of the 'fifties. The list is as follows:
1. Sanford's Opera Troupe—Philadelphia.
2. Ordway's Aeolians—Boston.
3. Wood's Minstrels—New York.
4. Campbell's Minstrels (Mat Peel, Manager).
5. Christy Minstrels (in Paris), part of the original company.
6. Campbell's Minstrels (Rumsey and Newcombe, Managers).
7. San Francisco Minstrels (California).
8. Buckley's Serenaders (a Travelling Company).
9. Bryant's Minstrels—New York.
10. George Christy and Hooley's Minstrels (Travelling).
11. Morris, Pell and Trowbridge's Minstrels—Boston.

The country was in the grip of the minstrel craze, and this genuinely American institution made an amazing appeal to all classes of the American people. New melodies for the minstrels, which appeared almost as rapidly as they could be printed and copyrighted, were quickly seized upon by the eager public, tried on the piano and other available instruments, and whistled on the streets. In many cities, in spite of the great number of new companies springing up each year, the rage for minstrelsy was so great that minstrel companies were forced to give morning concerts and "three-a-day" shows in order to satisfy the theatre-going public. During these years any good minstrel company could command the use of the best theatre in any city, filling it to capacity with little difficulty. In addition, many "nigger dancers," banjoists, and Ethiopian celebrities were performing individually, in the saloons and concert halls, with circuses and elephant shows, while the newspapers carried numerous references to the battles between rival banjoists or singers who sought to establish their claim to fame as the writers or introducers of some recent popular "song hit."

Producers of other kinds of amusements became greatly alarmed by the inroads made on their business by this new form of entertainment. One writer on stage affairs summarized the situation in the theatrical field as follows, "The great and increasing

popularity of Negro minstrelsy since its inaugura-
tion as a species of amusement, is a matter of serious concern to the purveyor of dramatic exhibi-
tions in every town or city upon the vast continent of
America. How frequently the most eminent in tragedy or comedy, have toiled through the choicest efforts, to scanty listeners; while upon the same evenings, fantazias upon the bones, or banjo, has *(sic)*
called forth the plaudits of admiring thousands."[34]
Another actor and producer lamented the collapse of
the drama in the 'forties, when the regular houses
were either entirely closed "or delivered over to jugglers, Negro singers, and the managers of such ob-
jects of low interest," and the public was being entertained by "ballet dancers, model artists, Hollick lec-
turers, Negro singers, Ethiopian serenaders, and
such like entertainments."[35] The *Evening Dispatch,*
of Augusta, Georgia, for February 5, 1858, reported
that a splendid company presenting *School for Scandal* in that city had no audience "in consequence of
the Campbell Minstrels,"[36] and the *Clipper* stated
that managers were "at a loss for novelties to buck
against that improving institution, Negro minstrelsy."[37] A production of *Monte Christo* failed to
attract satisfactory audiences in Richmond, Vir-

[34] Davidge, *op. cit.,* p. 127.
[35] William B. Wood, *Personal Recollections of the Stage* (Philadelphia, 1855), pp. 455, 465.
[36] Quoted in *The New York Clipper,* March 6, 1858.
[37] *The New York Clipper,* March 6, 1858.

ginia, until the enterprising manager engaged a band
of Ethiopian minstrels to play between acts.[38]  Minstrelsy had spread to England, to the Continent of
Europe, to Hawaii and Australia. "Travelling here
and there and everywhere, are bands almost in-
numerable, of every shade and quality." "Minstrelsy . . . has become a fixed institution, an im-
movable fact," commented the *Clipper* in 1860.
"While the drama is fast losing caste, the minstrelsy
business, on the other hand, is improving, the novelties and comicalities of our 'cullud brethren' crowd-
ing the houses nightly, the weather, whether good or
bad, making no difference."[39]

As the regular drama has suffered in more recent times by the competition of burlesque, vaudeville, movie houses, "girl shows," and "talkies," so
minstrelsy, by the middle of the nineteenth century,
was monopolizing the attention of the great majority
of American theatre-goers.  Little did the minstrel
managers, riding for several decades on the crest of
the wave of their great drawing power and prosperity, realize that within hardly more than two generations, they would be complaining bitterly against
newer forms of entertainment which were driving
the minstrel kings out of the professional field. Yet
today, the minstrels are almost "as dead as ole massa
and Uncle Ned."

[38] *The New York Clipper,* February 12, 1859.
[39] *Ibid.,* March 13, 1858, and March 17, 1860.

# CHAPTER III
## PROSPERITY AND DECLINE

The period from 1840 to 1870 is notable for many reasons in the history of the American theatre. At the beginning of the period, the actors appearing before American audiences were mainly of English birth and training. In many sections of the United States, the theatre, still somewhat in disrepute, was looked down upon by the eminently respectable as an immoral institution. Indeed, it was not until late in the 1850's, when thousands were drawn to the theatre to see *Uncle Tom's Cabin,* that the standing of the theatrical guild was considerably raised among the more Puritanically-minded. Even then a large portion of the religious people of the country considered theatre-going a sin, and the theatre "an unmitigated evil." As the country grew in size and its urban population increased, the theatre also assumed greater importance.

In the 'forties there were some fifty stock companies in the United States. Stars still traveled about as individual performers, relying upon local companies to furnish the supporting casts for their plays, and staying usually a week in each place. The cost of producing plays was mounting rapidly, especially because of the heavy salary demands made by star performers. Edwin Forrest dominated the

American stage throughout the period, Edwin Booth appeared in Boston in 1849, and Charlotte Cushman was enshrined in the hearts of American lovers of the drama. The charming Viennese dancer, Fanny Elssler arrived in the United States in 1840, William C. Macready, the English actor, came in 1849. New York's venture into the field of Italian opera failed in 1847 for lack of financial support, but in 1850, P. T. Barnum brought the Swedish Nightingale, Jenny Lind, to New York to begin her musical triumphs. Outside the large cities, the lecture, the concert, and the rapidly developing minstrel show were practically the only public amusements. The public lecture was at the height of its popularity during the decade preceding the Civil War. "Why should we regret it?" observed a prominent editor. "If people pay two shillings to see white men blackened like Negroes and singing maudlin sentiment, why should we not hope to see them paying the same sum to hear white men talk sense?"[1]

American theatres were of all descriptions from pretentious "marble palaces" to lowly and dingy halls of entertainment. The Bowery in New York, with its row of playhouses, was the predecessor of the Great White Way. Classical plays, with a special interest in Shakespeare, melodrama, native comedies, and minstrel shows were the main forms of enter-

[1] Quoted in James Ford Rhodes, *History of the United States* (New York, 1920), II, 547.

tainment. According to an English critic, who
landed in New York in 1869, "Negro minstrelsy was
still in its heyday, offering real melody and a humor
that was often genuine if always grotesque. It had
not yet been revolutionized and ruined by the 'mas-
todonic' notions of Jack Haverly."[2]

New York in 1870 had nearly a million people,
Philadelphia 750,000, Chicago 300,000 and Cincinnati 216,000. The growing number of large cities
and the rapid improvement of transportation facil-
ities served as a powerful stimulus to the theatrical
business during these years. Moreover, following
the close of the Civil War, the American public,
probably as a reaction from the strain of four years
of excitement and conflict, developed an unprece-
dented interest in all forms of public entertainment.
In New York, a Parisian ballet performed for seventeen months at Niblo's Garden and reaped a har-
vest of two hundred thousand dollars. In 1866, the
total receipts of the New York playhouses were estimated at between two and two and a half million dollars. Niblo's Garden alone had receipts of $350,000.
Theatres were beginning to be illuminated with
"gas-lights which will burn without wick or oil," and
in all the larger cities, "concert saloons," a new
amusement feature, stressing pretty waitresses and
catchy music, were coming in vogue. New York

[2] John Ranken Towse, *Sixty Years of the Theatre—An Old Critic's
Memories* (New York, 1916), p. 86.

City alone, in 1869, had six hundred of these "saloons." Needless to say, they varied all the way from beautiful and respectable music halls to the lowest saloons and dives.[3]

The generation of Americans following 1850 saw the heyday of Negro minstrelsy in the United States. This new form of entertainment reached its highest level in the decades from 1850 to 1870. Although some evidence can be found to show that the minstrel business was declining even before 1870, new companies continued to be organized after that date, many met with unusual success and some continued into the twentieth century. Early in the 1880's, there were at least thirty minstrel companies in existence at one time. For several decades after 1850, professional companies of burnt cork performers were permanently established in the theatres of the larger American cities, while many organizations were successful in their extensive tours of the country outside the great metropolitan centers. The close connection between the minstrels and the circus business, already pointed out, continued through these years, and many performers passed back and forth from the sawdust ring to the minstrel semicircle, lured by the larger salaries one or the other was temporarily able to offer. There was scarcely a

[3] See C. R. Fish, *The Rise of the Common Man* (New York, 1927), pp. 145-147; and Allen Nevins, *The Emergence of Modern America* (New York, 1927), pp. 93, 218.

circus, a street fair or a patent medicine show which did not carry one or more blackface performers among its entertainers, although the best artists naturally preferred the theatre. Even that craze for amateur minstrels which still makes this form of entertainment the favorite vehicle for the histrionic talents of church organizations, young business men's clubs, Rotarians, ladies' auxiliaries, and firemen's protective associations, became apparent soon after the close of the Civil War.[4]

With the development of railways and steam navigation during the latter half of the nineteenth century, the field for theatricals expanded enormously. Business men with surplus capital made investments in the amusement business, performances became more standardized and, under the lash of competition, were enlarged to suit the tastes "of a polyglot population that had money to spend on amusement and looked to business corporations to furnish it with the same facility with which they turned out bathtubs, shoes, hats and underwear."[5]

Minstrelsy like all other forms of entertaining the public, spread rapidly through the provinces, and the market for it expanded with the remarkably rapid development of new cities on what had been

[4] Gaines, op. cit., p. 96.
[5] Charles A. and Mary Beard, The Rise of American Civilization (New York, 1927), II, 774. In 1829, "overproduction" in the theatrical business of Philadelphia led to the bankruptcy of five theatres in that city. Ibid., I, 795.

but recently the farmer's frontier. It was in this great period of national expansion that minstrelsy found at once its greatest prosperity as well as the forces that were slowly to lead to its disintegration and eventual collapse. For as minstrelsy prospered, the character of minstrel productions changed radically, performers drifted farther and farther away from the prototypes on which their art originally had been based, and with the insatiable demand of the American public for "bigger and better" minstrels, salaries and the costs of management and production finally reached the point where financial success became almost impossible.

As suggested in the preceding chapter, scores of new minstrel organizations made their appearance in the American theatrical world in the 1850's and 1860's. New York City alone had at least ten halls or theatres in which the minstrels held forth in the 1850's. Three companies were playing on Broadway, on the same side of the street and within a few doors of each other.[6] The Minerva Rooms, at 460 Broadway, opened in 1847, was the scene of many famous minstrel performances. At 472 Broadway stood the famous Mechanics Hall, opened in 1847 by Christy's company and destined to house that organization for almost a decade. When this company at last relinquished the theatre which it had

[6] Rice, *Memories of the Minstrels* (a broadside) (New York, 1913).

made famous, White's Minstrels took possession. The Fellow's Opera House and Hall of Lyrics, which stood at 444 Broadway, was opened by a band of minstrels, and in 1853, was renamed Christy and Wood's Minstrel Hall. Other New York halls occupied by minstrel companies during the 1850's were Old Stuyvesant Hall, later known as Academy Hall, Mozart Hall, Niblo's Saloon, and the Union Concert Hall. In 1851, the Coliseum, at 448 Broadway, was opened by minstrels, and Hope Chapel, once a church and located on Broadway near Eighth Street, became the Academy of Minstrels in 1856. A decade later, Kelly and Leon's Theatre, owned by one of the best known minstrel troupes of the time, was opened to the public with high-priced minstrelsy offered at a dollar and a half admission. White's Opera House, at 49 Bowery, was opened by Charles White's company in 1854. Buckley's Hall, dedicated in 1856, was renamed the San Francisco Minstrel Hall in 1865. Henry Wood's Marble Hall, constructed partly of marble, as its name implied, and seating two thousand, stood at 561 Broadway. It was devoted to minstrel performances and concerts in 1857, and for many years thereafter. Wood's Minstrel Hall, at 514 Broadway, was a Jewish synagogue remodeled into a minstrel theatre. Bryant's Minstrel Hall, one of the most famous theatres ever devoted to burnt cork art, stood at Fourteenth

Street, and was opened by Bryant's Minstrels in 1868.[7] Wood's Minstrels appeared in Barnum's Museum nightly and every afternoon during the summer of 1860.[8] Hooley and Campbell's Opera House at 585 Broadway featured a minstrel company with Billy Birch, just returned from California, as their star. Later, the same company announced the leasing of Niblo's Saloon for the entire winter of 1860-1861, "for a series of Ethiopian Entertainments in the most *recherché* style."[9] During the preceding winter, George Christy's Minstrels had held forth for weeks at Niblo's with frequent changes of program. The manager showed remarkable resourcefulness in the creation of new farces, some of which were burlesques of recent happenings in world affairs, and the hall continued to be "crowded with the Elite and Beauty of the City."[10]

The panic of 1857 seems to have had little effect upon the spread of minstrelsy. While all other forms of amusement seemed to be suffering from the economic depression, the "cullud opera" was multiplying. Indeed, the closing years of the 1850's showed remarkable activity in the minstrel field. The Prendergast Minstrels opened at the new Olympic Theatre on Broadway, New York, in 1857, with a

[7] See Dimmick, *op. cit.*, pp. 34-48, and Brown, *History of the New York Stage*, I, 408.

[8] *New York Tribune*, August 14, 1860.

[9] *Ibid.*, August 14, 27, 1860.

[10] *Ibid.*, January 2; February 9, 17, 27; April 14; June 13, 1860.

pretentious array of performers including T. B. Prendergast, J. H. Budworth, Charley White, J. Carrol, H. Stephens, J. Barker, H. Troutman, H. Wilson, T. Norton, J. Waddee, L. Donnelly, W. W. Snow, and others.[11] Christy's Minstrels had sailed for Europe just three months earlier.[12] Bryant's Minstrels were thriving at 472 Broadway, with a distinguished company of thirteen performers, featuring a program of songs, dances, "burlesque sayings," Shakespearian readings, sawdust acrobats, a challenge dance and other varieties.[13] The following year, Wood's Minstrels with a "rare combination of Ethiopian talents" which included Daddy Rice, Eph Horn, Charley White and other stars, were reporting excellent business in New York.[14] Budworth's Minstrels, a little show that played to a ten-cent admission charge, was at Sixteenth Street and Eighth Avenue.[15]

In 1870, Dan Bryant opened Bryant's Opera House on Twenty-third Street, near Sixth Avenue. Bryant's Minstrels played continuously for nine years at Mechanics Hall, eight months in San Francisco, and then returned to other New York theatres for a total run of sixteen years, a record which it would be difficult to duplicate in all the annals of the

[11] *The New York Clipper,* October 24, 1857.
[12] *Ibid.,* July 18, 1857.
[13] *Ibid.,* February 28, June 27, 1857.
[14] *Ibid.,* August 14, 1858.
[15] *Ibid.,* March 6, 1858.

American stage. Wood's Minstrels played at one hall or another in New York City for a total of fifteen years, and Hooley's Minstrels played in Brooklyn for a decade. As late as 1872, there were four minstrel companies playing in New York. Another San Francisco Minstrel Hall was opened on Broadway, between Twenty-eighth and Twenty-ninth Street, in 1875. In 1883, it passed under the control of J. H. Haverly, and three years later, was reopened as Dockstader's Minstrel Hall where Dockstader's company had a phenomenal run of three years. Aberle's Theatre, on Eighth Street between Broadway and Fourth Avenue, a remodelled Roman Catholic church, was opened to minstrel performances in 1879.[16] The old Bowery Theatre, for years one of the leading, and certainly among the most picturesque, theatres in the metropolis, with a record running back to the days of Washington and the first in New York to be lighted by gas, was the scene of numerous minstrel performances. After the Civil War, "Negro minstrels of the lowest order" continued to visit this ancient landmark, whose gallery audiences seemed to be particularly notorious for their "depravity and degradation."[17]

Boston was another important minstrel center. Indeed, M. B. Leavitt, an actor and theatrical man-

[16] Dimmick, op. cit., pp. 53, 56.
[17] See Herbert Asbury, "The Old-Time Gangs of New York." The American Mercury, August, 1927, pp. 478-486.

ager for fifty years, maintained that Boston was the place of origin of more burnt cork shows than the rest of the country combined. Although this undoubtedly is an exaggeration, the statement throws light on the very considerable interest New England had in this form of theatrical entertainment. As a matter of fact, before the close of the 'forties, minstrel companies like the Diamond Minstrels, the Ethiopian Minstrels, the Sable Harmonists, the Guinea Minstrels, and several sets of Ethiopian Entertainers and Serenaders had made their début in Boston. Buckley's Minstrels gave an entertainment at the old Masonic Temple of Boston in 1843, and Thayer and Newcomb's company performed there also. In 1846, Jerry Merrifield's minstrel band was at the old Adelphi Theatre, while Murphy, West and Peel's Minstrels and Dumbolton's Serenaders appeared before the close of the decade.

During the 1850's and 1860's, the New England metropolis was noted as a minstrel rendezvous. Numerous juvenile minstrel companies, like the Young Campbells and Leavitt's Alabama Minstrels and Nightingale Serenaders were launched in Boston as a new experiment in burnt cork attractions.[18] Ordway's Aeolians and Melodists played in Harmony Hall, Boston, for two years, beginning in December, 1850. Thereupon they moved to a new hall, which

[18] Leavitt, *op. cit.*, pp. 25, 26. The same author lists seventy-eight minstrel companies established since 1843. *Ibid.*, pp. 29-30.

they occupied to 1859, and finally sold their holdings
to the Morris Brothers, Pell and Trowbridge Minstrels.[19]  P. S. Gilmore, famous bandmaster, played
the cornet in Ordway's show in 1852, in a program
featuring songs, burlesques, dances, bone and accordeon solos and banjo duets.

In the 1850's, numerous minstrel troupes played
in Hartford, Connecticut, including Buckley's Serenaders, Matt Peel's Campbell Minstrels, Rumsey and
Newcomb's, and many others.  In addition, the town
supported a local minstrel company.[20]  The first minstrel theatre was opened in Philadelphia in 1853, and
from 1855 to 1862, Sam S. Sanford's Minstrels occupied the Eleventh Street Opera House in that city,
and the Carncross and Dixey Minstrels ran for nine
years at the Continental Theatre.  In Cincinnati,
Pike's Opera House, the city's finest hall, built by
a public-spirited German Jew whose real name was
Hecht, was the favorite theatre of traveling companies.

By 1850 minstrelsy was well established in the
Middle West and other sections of the United States.
Ohio will serve as a typical state for this period.  The
Buckeye Minstrels, founded in Springfield, Ohio,
made their first appearance at the Melodeon in Cin-
cinnati, on January 7, 1850, and played to capacity

[19] *Ibid.*, pp. 23, 25.  Also, *Boston Minstrelsy*, in the Allen A. Brown
collection of books on the stage, Boston Public Library.
[20] Leavitt, *op. cit.*, p. 20.

houses. Outstanding features of the show were
"The Alpine .Echo," "a superb specimen of harmony," and the ballad entitled "The Angel's Whisper."[21] In the following month, the company gave
its "concerts" at the Odeon in Columbus, where
"their gentlemanly bearing and fine musical taste"
made them many friends.[22] Another company,
known as The Empire Minstrels, and hailing originally from Buffalo, opened in Cincinnati in March,
1850. It consisted of ten actors, featuring "a champion dancer" and Cool White, "the renowned Shakespearean Negro jester." On March 26, the company moved to Columbus, after fifty-one performo
ances in Pittsburgh and twenty-four consecutive
shows in Cincinnati. The company appeared in citizen's dress and in white face in the first part, and
as Ethiopians in the second and third parts of the
program. Press notices were very favorable.[23] On
March 9, The Original Washington Euterpeans
opened in Cincinnati at the Melodeon, and announced
four "of their chaste and inimitable Vocal and Instrumental entertainments" for an admission of
thirty cents.[24] The Ethiopian Serenaders played in
Columbus early the following year, after thirty successive nights in Cincinnati.[25]

[21] *Cincinnati Gazette*, January 7, 1850.
[22] *Ohio State Journal*, February 5 and 7, 1850.
[23] See *Cincinnati Gazette*, March 6, 16, 22, 1850; and *Ohio State Journal*, March 26 and 28, 1850.
[24] *Cincinnati Gazette*, March 4 and 9, 1850.
[25] *Ohio State Journal*, February 25, 1851.

In August, 1851, a Harmoneon Troupe performed at the Melodeon in Cleveland. "Nothing transpired which could possibly mar the most fastidious taste."[26] The preceding month, R. Gray's Ethiopian Warblers, a company of eight, had presented "Burlesques of the Dutch Malicious Drill," "Black Shakers," and "Swiss Bell Ringers, or Warbler's Cowbellogians."[27] Before the close of the season, Horn, Wells and Briggs' Ethiopian Serenaders also played in Cleveland, but the two local papers could not agree as to the merits of the performers or whether the audience was composed of gentlemen or rowdies.[28] During 1853, Columbus was visited by Kunkel's Nightingales who for three nights presented "songs of high character" and a Negro part of the program which was "less disgusting than usual."[29] In the preceding month, Kunkel's Nightingales had played in Smith and Nixon's Concert Hall in Cincinnati, excelling all other companies, "as Jenny Lind excels ordinary vocalists." George Kunkel especially was praised for his singing of "The Old Sexton."[30] In the same city, Campbell's Minstrels played during April, and Wells' Minstrels ran for six months consecutively, finally securing control of the Melodeon, which was renamed Wells'

[26] *Cleveland Daily Herald,* August 13, 14, 1851.
[27] *Ibid.,* July 21, 1851.
[28] *Ibid.,* November 4, 1851.
[29] *Ohio State Journal,* April 11, 1853.
[30] *Cincinnati Gazette,* March 21, 1853.

Ethiopian Opera House.[31]   In the late summer of
1855, a concert troupe of considerable reputation
and excellence had to give its concerts in the morning, because every available hall and theatre of Cincinnati was occupied by minstrel companies.[32]

Campbell's Minstrels, with a specially augmented
company featuring Eph Horn and W. W. Newcomb,
played to full houses in Ohio's capital city during
the summer of 1853.   The "Negro witticisms" contained "less objectionable allusions than is usual,"
and the music, dancing and burlesque gymnastics
were considered of special excellence.   The reporter
of the *Ohio State Journal,* however, complained because "the door-keeper was puffing a cigar in the
face of all who entered the hall."[33]   In December,
Dumbolton's Metropolitan Serenaders, "the Ne Plus
Ultra of Ethiopian Minstrels" with the renowned
Cool White, appeared in Columbus, featuring songs,
operatic burlesques, glees, dancing, Ethiopian melodies and Shakespearean readings.   In February,
1856, Brown's Nightingale Opera Troupe presented
"original Ethiopian Concerts"[34] and the following
year, The Apollo Minstrels, advertised as the "only
original Negroes travelling," were giving "three of
their popular and original *Soirees de Ethiope*" in

[31] *Cincinnati Gazette,* January 29, April 19, 1853.
[32] *Ibid.,* September 11, 1855.
[33] *Ohio State Journal,* August 29, 1853.
[34] *Ibid.,* February 1, 1856.

Columbus.[35]   Other troupes visiting Ohio in the 1850's were the Christy Minstrels, Mason's Metropolitan Serenaders, Birch's Minstrels, and Birch and Oak's Minstrels.   The brightest stars on the Ohio Minstrel stage during this period seem to have been Sliter, "the most brilliant dancer of the day," Cool White, Kunkel, and Mike Mitchell, "the never-was-outdone dancer of the present age."[36]   The regular admission charge for minstrel shows in Ohio, as elsewhere, was twenty-five cents during this period.[37]

With the gold rush of 1849, minstrelsy leaped over the thousand miles of vacant lands dividing the first tier of states west of the Mississippi from the settlements on the Pacific coast, and invaded the new-born California towns and mining camps.   An Australian troupe playing *Othello,* and a French vaudeville company offering a more boisterous form of entertainment, were among the first theatrical organizations to arrive on the Pacific coast to amuse the miners and their camp followers in the newly constructed wooden theatres of California.[38]   The San Francisco Minstrels followed closely on the heels of these earliest theatrical ventures, and in a short time, several theatres in the boom town of San Francisco were given over entirely to minstrelsy.

[35] *Ohio State Journal,* January 17, 1857.

[36] See *Ohio State Journal,* March 28, 1850, and *Cincinnati Gazette,* April 10, 1854.

[37] *Ohio State Journal,* December 10, 1853.

[38] Beard, *op. cit.,* I, 795. .

With the completion of the first transcontinental
railroad in 1869, minstrelsy invaded many of the
western towns along the route. It was in the summer of 1869, for example, that Murphy and Mack's
Minstrels delighted large audiences for ten days in
the famous Salt Lake Theatre of the Mormons of
Utah. Two years later, the Joe Murphy of this
minstrel troupe returned to the Mormon capital as
an Irish comedian.[39]

Among the minstrel favorites of the Pacific
Coast were Ben Cotton, a song and dance man,
Charley Backus, of the famous Birch, Bernard,
Wambold and Backus combination (an organization
which made its début on the west coast as the San
Francisco Minstrels), Joe Murphy, a bone player
and singer at auctions and cheap entertainments in
Sacramento who had risen to the distinction of being
the champion bone player of the Pacific Coast and
later went into Irish comedy, and Johnny de Angeles,
father of the better known Jefferson de Angeles.
Among the balladists of the early San Francisco
minstrel days were Dave Wambold, advertised in
later years as "the sweet tenor of the old San Francisco Minstrels," Henri Herbert, Tom Casselli,
Tommy Bree and J. G. Russell. The latter was
traveling under an assumed name and it was generally believed that he had killed his man in the East,

[39] George D. Pyper, *The Romance of an Old Playhouse* (Salt Lake
City, 1928), pp. 171-172.

presumably in self-defence. In the new West he
earned an honest living with his rich baritone, and
in songs like "You and I" and "We Parted by the
Riverside" melted the hearts of his California audiences. Billy Ashcraft and Dick Sands, one of the
best "cloggers" in the United States, were among
the earliest song and dance teams in San Francisco;
and to Johnny Tuers generally was conceded the
honor of being the champion flat foot dancer on the
west coast.

Another interesting character in this group of
early California minstrel luminaries was Fred
Sprung, a native German, who served as bass soloist and interlocutor. He began his career as a singer
and actor on a show boat of the Mississippi, known
as the River Boat Minstrels. Lew Rattler, a San
Francisco favorite for twenty-five years, excelled as
a singer and end man, and as a writer of burlesque
opera. The San Francisco Minstrels played not only
on the Pacific Coast, but appeared in New York,
Australia and New Zealand as well. Birch, Wambold
and Backus in their New York appearance made a
special effort to make minstrelsy more refined and to
adhere as rigidly as possible to real plantation
models, relying on simple settings, beautiful ballads
and real Negro comedy for their success. In the
late 1860's, Billy Emerson and Charley Howard, two
of the greatest balladists minstrelsy has produced,

appeared on the San Francisco stage. The former, endowed with a rich tenor voice, made his songs like "Love Among the Roses" and "The Big Sunflower" extremely popular, while the latter sang old melodies like "Old Black Joe" and spirituals like "Go Down Moses" with peculiar effect and success. In May, 1871, The San Francisco Minstrels made their first appearance in Chicago before a capacity house. The old combination still was practically intact. Birch and Backus played the ends, Bernard was interlocutor, Wambold was featured as a balladist, and Rollin Howard won great applause as a performer of Negro dances and character songs.[40]

Thus, by the time of the Civil War, minstrelsy not only had extraordinary vogue, but apparently had permanent possession of many theatres in at least a half dozen of the larger cities, while road companies had carried the blackface art across the open spaces of the west and were enjoying unusual prosperity on the new California frontier.

Scores of companies by this time were touring all the "provinces." During the summer of 1857, Rumsey and Newcomb's Campbell Minstrels reached Mobile, Alabama; Mat Peel's Campbell Minstrels traveled from Cleveland to New Orleans, and Dick

[40] *The New York Clipper,* June 10, 1871. For minstrelsy on the Pacific Coast see, Brown, *History of the American Stage,* p. 62; *Literary Digest,* August 16, 1919, p. 29; and E. T. Sawyer, "Old Time Minstrels of San Francisco," in *Overland,* October, 1923, pp. 5-8.

Sliter's troupe was touring Ohio. Sharpley's Minstrels were in Kansas and Nebraska, although in these days of the bitter sectional controversy over "Bleeding Kansas," "the 'nigger business' had been pretty well used up in that section."[41] The following year, Matt Peel's troupe reached Savannah; Dan Emmett and Fred Lumbard had organized a new show in St. Paul; Sanford's Ethiopian Troupe was holding forth in Chicago; May's Campbell Minstrels visited Wheeling; the Birch, Bowers and Fox's Minstrels were playing to profitable houses in the St. Louis Museum, and Sweeney and Company's Virginia Minstrels and Landis's Minstrels were in the national capital. The Steamboat Minstrels opened in Mobile, early in 1858.[42] In 1859 Wells and Hussey's Minstrels and Wells and Coes' Minstrels were in California; two companies, Fred Judson's Minstrels and The Uncle Sam Troupe were performing in Indianapolis; Wood's New York Minstrels were at Yazoo City en route for New Orleans; Birch and Donniker's Minstrels were in St. Louis; Beler's Campbell Minstrels in Iowa; Charley Sanford and Smith's Minstrels in Louisville; and one of Leavitt's new companies was opening in Hartford, Connecticut. Putnam, Wright and Master's Ethiopian Troupe advertised itself in Maine as "the most tal-

[41] See *The New York Clipper*, especially October 31, 10, 24, 1857.
[42] *Ibid.*, January 16, 23, May 28, June 5, September 25, October 2, November 20, December 11, 1858.

ented company ever organized," and the Campbell
Sable Brothers Minstrels were prospering in New
Haven.[43]   Hooley and Campbell's Minstrels, early
in 1860, were doing an excellent business in Chicago,
reporting receipts of over fifteen hundred dollars in
six nights.[44]   The Christy Minstrels, back in New
York from their European triumphs, advertised
poetically, and truthfully, "Be the weather foul or
fair, hundreds gather there; to see the fun, to hear
the songs, and help to right the 'niggers' ' wrongs."[45]

Minstrelsy was indeed prosperous, so prosperous
that competition between the performers and the various companies was exceedingly keen and bitter.
The theatrical papers of the 'fifties and 'sixties are
full of accounts of the break-up of old companies and
the secession of stars from their old managers.
There were so many breaches of contracts with
furious bidding for the services of the most popular
performers, that it became "almost as difficult to
manage the cullud Opera as the Italian."[46]   Warn-
ings were inserted in the newspapers and theatrical
journals, so that the public might not be misled into
patronizing rival companies, instead of the "original."[47]

[43] *The New York Clipper,* February 5, 26, March 5, May 14, 21,
December 31, 1859.

[44] *Ibid.,* April 7, 1860.

[45] *Ibid.,* December 24, 1859.

[46] *Ibid.,* October 9, 1858.

[47] *Ibid.,* February 25, March 3, 1860.

At the outbreak of war in 1861, some companies came to grief in the South. There, as in other parts of the country, they found it difficult to adjust their program of songs and comedy to the tastes of the excited public and to the conflicting viewpoints concerning the war and secession which they encountered among their various audiences. Although minstrelsy always enjoyed its greatest vogue in the South, some companies encountered considerable trouble in their efforts to get back to the North after the Civil War had begun. Duprez and Green's Minstrels, who happened to be playing in New Orleans when the war began with the firing on Fort Sumter, were forced to make all possible speed in their trip northward. At Charleston, South Carolina, where George Christy's Minstrels were performing, the manager had to explain in a curtain speech to the audience that he had no sympathy with the Union cause. One morning, on coming to the theatre for rehearsal, the company had found a Palmetto tree drawn on the wall near the rear stage entrance, with the inscription, "Death to the Yankees." At Wilkesbarre, Pennsylvania, Bishop and Florence's Minstrels encountered trouble because two members of the troupe were Southerners. With unusual indiscretion, they engaged in an argument with some of the excited townspeople about the issues of the war and the merits of secession. A mob stormed the

theatre after the performance and the actors were
forced to leap from their dressing room windows in
order to escape serious injury.  Distorted tales of the
incident soon were in circulation all over the state,
and the minstrel business suffered throughout Pennsylvania as a result of this unfortunate incident.
On the other hand, a clever advertising manager for
one of the shows, La Rue's Minstrels, greatly increased the box office receipts in many Northern
cities by circulating the "hoax" that one of the star
performers had been shot in Montreal for uphold-
ing the Union cause.[48]

In spite of difficulties of this sort, the theatres
remained open in the North during the war and were
reasonably well attended.  Minstrel comedians were
quick to discover what alterations had to be made
in their lines and what new songs had to be introduced into the first part to satisfy their patriotic
audiences.  In the Southern Confederacy, also, the
theatres remained open in some places until as late
as 1865.  In Richmond, for example, just before its
surrender in 1865, Budd and Buckley's Minstrels
and Brass Band were "received nightly with shouts
of applause."  As eloquent testimony of the increasing effectiveness of the federal blockade of
Southern ports, the company announced that it
would pay the highest price for old and new cork, if

[48] Leavitt, op. cit., pp. 73-74; Charles H. Day, Fun in Black
(Harper's, New York, 1874), pp. 16, 42.

presented at the hall. Apparently, the Confederate authorities fully approved of theatres remaining open as long as possible during the war. They provided recreation for wounded soldiers and, perhaps, served to keep others out of mischief.[49]

In the decade of the 'seventies, with only a temporary interruption caused by the panic of 1873, the theatre had a particularly brilliant history in the United States. That intense activity which characterized America in the years following the close of the great sectional struggle between North and South also manifested itself by a renewed interest and activity in theatrical matters. By the close of the decade, native American plays had largely superseded the European importations of earlier years, and were much more popular. A new type of theatrical manager developed also, in line with the new philosophy of "big business" resulting from the Economic Revolution. The theatre manager tried to emulate the methods of his contemporary in the business world by seeking means to end the cut-throat competition between theatres through fraternal combinations and "gentlemen's agreements" among owners and managers and by emphasizing "bigger and better" stage offerings.

The theatres themselves, with a few notable exceptions like Booth's Million Dollar Palace, were

[49] Rhodes, op. cit., V, 116.

still for the most part rather plain structures, seating
from four to fifteen hundred people, with a typical
high dome in the center, walls of showy plate glass
lining the vestibules, and the auditorium proper divided into a pit, one or more galleries, and tiers
of boxes on each side. Salaries of actors still were
low, thirty-five dollars a week being considered excellent pay. At the close of each season it was customary to give a series of "benefits" for actors, authors and managers, and the public was asked to
give tangible evidence of its appreciation of the season's work by patronizing these special performances. As the show business prospered, the playing season in a number of cities was extended well
into the summer. It often came to a glorious end on
the Fourth of July with a patriotic demonstration,
the companies closing with "thrillers" like *The
Man of Destiny, Blanche of Brandywine,* or *Our
Country's Flag.*

By the 1870's, the minstrel show was changing
rapidly into something like a "tired business man's
show," the forerunner of present day burlesque,
movies, and follies shows. New companies continued to be organized, most of them seeming to
prosper. A number were supported and financed
by the notorious "Coal Oil Johnny," who had become wealthy suddenly in the Pennsylvania oil fields
and was looking for new fields of investment. After

he had lost his fortune by a series of bad theatrical ventures, he found employment for a short time as advance agent for a minstrel show.

The vogue of minstrelsy seemed as great as ever and by no means was it confined to the more densely populated Eastern centers. A musical locality like Cincinnati, for example, had the same full quota of minstrel productions during the 1870's, as two decades earlier. Its minstrel season for 1870 opened with The World-Renowned Arlington Minstrels at Mozart Hall, an aggregation of twenty-one performers including William Arlington, "the greatest living Ethiopian delineator," Sam Price, "the inimitable Sable Humorist," Sam Sidney, "the famous Burlesque Character and Protean Actor," and the sensational Chang, the Chinese Giant.[50] Newcomb's Minstrels, "the acme of excellence," played for three nights in February at Pike's Music Hall. This company also advertised as a special feature the *real* Chang, "standing over eight feet high . . . accompanied by his Wife, 'King Foo,' the Golden Lily, and Most Beautiful of Chinese Women," and furiously denounced the humbug perpetrated "by an unprincipled manager" (obviously Arlington) who had visited Cincinnati with his company during the preceding month. The Chinese Giant was expected to draw the curious to the minstrel performance, and

[50] *Cincinnati Daily Gazette,* January 15, 1870.

visitors to "Chang's Levees" during the day were admitted upon the ticket to the evening minstrel performance. On a previous visit this enterprising manager had used a lottery device, by which he distributed bundles of one hundred dollars in greenbacks, to draw the Cincinnati crowds into his theatre.[51] The reporter of the *Cincinnati Gazette* wrote a scathing review. He found that the wit of the minstrels "was not attic," the stories and conundrums "veterans . . . that deserve now to be buried," some songs badly rendered, the sketches "mournful failures," and the concluding Negro extravaganza "quite melancholy."[52]

In April, Allen and Pettengill's Sensation Minstrels, and the excellent Emerson Minstrels each ran four nights at Mozart Hall. During the same season, Manning's Minstrels remained for four weeks at Wood's Theatre.[53] The same theatre, in July, entertained Skiff and Gaylord's Gigantic Minstrel Troupe, a company of twenty-five, including "a matchless quintette, a grand Triple Clog, and a wonderful Panithiopliconica."[54] Emerson's troupe played a return engagement in the fall of 1870 and offended some of their audience by the low moral tone of the new program. Emerson, a real Cincin-

[51] *Cincinnati Daily Gazette*, February 12, 1870.
[52] *Ibid.*, February 15, 1870.
[53] *Ibid.*, April 13, 18, May 25, 1870.
[54] *Ibid.*, July 22, 1870.

nati favorite, promptly was reminded "that he can not afford to play at the galleries, unless he wishes to see the lower part of the house empty or tenanted only by roughs." Emerson took the advice to heart and in a few days he was advertising "a new, chaste, and pleasing performance." After a run of several weeks, the company gave a benefit for Billy Emerson, prior to his departure for California, Australia and China.[55]

Bryant's Minstrels also visited Cincinnati in the summer of 1870 and played at Pike's Hall. The program perhaps deserves special mention, because it shows clearly how variety acts were becoming regular features of even the best minstrel performances. After a more or less traditional first part, Dan Bryant, as conductor *a la Maretzek,* presented a concert, featuring Eugene, the wonderful burlesque prima donna. In a character act, entitled "The Drum Major," Dan Bryant displayed his unusual skill as a manipulator of the bones. There followed a farce, a burlesque duet by Bryant and Griffin of *Gens d'Armes,* a stump speech, a banjo solo, and an act called "Daniel in the Bryant's den." The next number was the famous "Shoo Fly," as "vitalized and made a public necessity of by Dan Bryant and Dave Reed," a song given by these two stars for at least two hundred and fifty nights on Broad-

[55] *Cincinnati Daily Gazette,* October 24, 25, 26; November 4, 9, 1870.

way. The program closed with another comic act and the burlesque opera, "Ill-True-Bad-Doer," with Eugene singing the principal female rôle.[56] During this Cincinnati engagement, other burlesque operas, like "Lucretia Borgia," "Somnambula," "Girl of the Period," and Dan Bryant's "Hamlet" were introduced from week to week.[57] Johnny Allen's Minstrels were playing in St. Louis in the fall of 1870, while Simmons and Slocum's Minstrels were presenting "A soul-harrowing burlesque on East Lynne" in Philadelphia.[58] In the spring of 1871, Newcomb and Arlington's Minstrels opened at the Twenty-eighth Street Opera House in New York with a new feature known as "Walter Bray's Corkographics."[59]

The disastrous panic which affected the entire country in 1873 and brought on a half dozen years of suffering and depression in the west and south, naturally created considerable disturbance for a time in the theatrical business. In the season of 1873-1874, eighteen out of thirty-nine minstrel companies on the road failed.[60] But since the eastern section of the United States recovered much more rapidly from this economic depression than the agricultural west and south, in a short time minstrelsy,

[56] *Cincinnati Daily Gazette,* July 20, 1870.
[57] *Ibid.,* July 14, 19, 1870.
[58] *Ibid.,* October 8, 1870.
[59] *The New York Clipper,* June 10, 1871.
[60] Paskman and Spaeth, *op. cit.,* p. 5; and Day, *op. cit.,* p. 59.

as well as the theatre business in general, had regained most of the lost ground, especially in the eastern states.

During the season of 1875, Duprez and Benedict's Minstrels, an organization of twenty-eight performers, visited Cleveland twice, playing an engagement at Brainard's Opera House in April, and a second at the Academy of Music three months later.[61] Happy Cal Wagner's Minstrels made two visits to the same city, the first in February and the second late in August, 1875.[62] Haverly's company came to Brainard's Opera House in February, following an engagement in Cincinnati. The papers of both Ohio towns were agreed in their praise of this organization as the "best minstrel troupe traveling." The company apparently carried some excellent vocal talent, for Primrose and West were featured as "the *ne plus ultra* of song and dance," while Adam Kunz appeared as the champion banjo player and received a ring from his many Cleveland admirers. The *Cincinnati Enquirer* was especially delighted with D. L. Morris, "the black Dutchman" who was "infinitely ludicrous in his murdering and misapplication of the Queen's English."[63] In the fall season of 1875, Bryant's Minstrels, with a company of twenty-four, appeared for two nights at the Globe Theatre in

[61] *Cleveland Plain Dealer,* April 29, July 7, 1875.
[62] *Ibid.,* February 8, August 31, 1875.
[63] *Ibid.,* February 10, 1875.

Cleveland. Admission charges to the performances of this high-class company ranged from twenty-five to seventy-five cents.[64]

Colored performers also were much in demand during the 'seventies. It was a decade when the North was deeply interested in the problem of Southern reconstruction arising from the Civil War, and in the future of the freedmen. The Fisk Jubilee Singers toured not only America, but Europe during this decade, and introduced a new type of Negro music to the audiences of two continents. Collections of "jubilee songs," introduced by the Fisk University singers of Nashville and issued by Biglow and Main in New York, in 1872, achieved an immediate and unique popularity. Enterprising managers after assembling companies of plantation Negroes, presented them in Ethiopian concerts in many of the Northern states. During the late fall of 1875 the North Carolinians, for example, appeared in Case Hall, Cleveland, in slave costume, playing "upon the rude instruments of the South," such as jaw bones and shells. The reviewer of the *Plain Dealer* described them as "a company of genuine field hands from the Southern plantations, male and female, who were formerly slaves. Their music is the weird, grotesque, but generally melodious music of the plantation," a "ruder and more literal"

[64] *Cleveland Plain Dealer,* October 19, 1875.

portrayal of the Southern Negro music than given by the Jubilee singers of Fisk and Hampton.[65] At the Theatre Comique, another Cleveland playhouse, the Colored Hamtown Singers sang their Negro melodies;[66] a dozen Jubilee Singers from Jackson, Tennessee, described as "weird choristers," appeared at Brainard's Opera House in "old time melodies, camp meeting hymns, Southern scenes and grand tableaux."[67] Callender's Original Georgia Minstrels, advertised as "the great Southern slave troupe," with four end men who were "uproarious plantation delineators," came to the Cleveland Academy of Music, with the alleged endorsement of William Lloyd Garrison, Oliver Wendell Holmes, James Russell Lowell and P. T. Barnum.[68] A decade later, the successors to this troupe, Henderson's Colored Minstrels, were performing at the People's Theatre in Cincinnati, at admissions of ten to thirty cents. The company remained here a whole week, featuring a traditional first part, a second part opened by John Armstrong, "the Alabama Slave," who imitated steam calliopes, planing mills and dogs, and lifted chairs and tables with his powerful jaw; a farce entitled "Clarinda's Lovers"; and "Life on the Old Plantation" as the closing act.[69]

[65] *Cleveland Plain Dealer, December* 9, 13, 1875.
[66] *Ibid.,* June 14, 1875.
[67] *Ibid.,* February 25, 1875.
[68] *Ibid.,* December 11, 1875.
[69] *The Cincinnati Enquirer,* May 3, 1885.

In 1877, Harry Bloodgood's Minstrels, after opening a season in Boston, perfected a plan to travel with a caravan of horses and wagons to all the small towns of New England not easily accessible by railroad.[70] Kelly and Leon's Minstrels, during the same season, played for a whole week "to a very fair business" in Cincinnati, while Haverly's Minstrels were in their third week in Chicago.[71] Finally, in 1879, when conditions in the theatrical world had reached complete normalcy again, the *New York Dramatic Mirror,* in a summary of dramatic affairs in Philadelphia, commented with considerable truth, "neither Modjeska, nor Clara Morris, nor Fanny Davenport, nor any other star that has flashed across the sky this season has drawn such a multitude of people as came to see Haverly's Mastodon Minstrels."[72]

Before discussing the great minstrel companies of later days, it may be well to include here a summary of the reminiscences of an old-time minstrel manager and performer, who, in the 1860's, toured with a road company through the state of Maine and the British North American Provinces. He wrote an account of his experiences many years later for the *Boston Commercial Bulletin,* a copy of which fortunately has been preserved in the Allen A. Brown collection of books on the stage in the Boston

[70] *The New York Clipper,* September 29, 1877.
[71] *Ibid.*
[72] Quoted in Gaines, *op. cit.,* p. 102.

Public Library.[73] The experiences of this New England minstrel must have been typical of the period when scores of little companies toured the rural sections of the country, before minstrelsy had been commercialized and developed to "gigantean, mastodon" proportions.

The writer of these interesting reminiscences was the younger son of a medical doctor living in one of the suburbs of Boston. After graduating from the Boston Latin School, the adventurous youth disobeyed the wishes of his parents, refused to enter college, and instead, joined a minstrel company. The organization was only a small one, with a salary roll not exceeding $250 a week for the entire company of thirteen or fourteen performers and musicians. Troupes of this kind seldom had the courage to face the audiences of metropolitan New York or Boston. Their programs were planned to please their rural patrons, the mechanics and farmers of the smaller towns, who, dazzled by the gaudy posters pasted by the advance agent on every "dead wall" or barn, were easily persuaded to part with twenty-five cents in order to hear the latest jokes, see the newest dance steps and learn the latest ballads, dripping with sentiment and touchingly rendered by the company's

[73] *Negro Minstrelsy, the Old Fashioned Troupes* (Boston, 189-), 16 pp.

"silver-toned tenor."[74]  A company of this size seldom carried stage-carpenters or scene-shifters; usually there were no scenes or other stage paraphernalia to transport. · Each performer furnished and carried his own "wardrobe," consisting of a wig, a "first-part suit," with "clawhammer" coat, vest and trousers to match, paper collars and scarf, and some weird costume for the olio, with grotesque shoes.

It was in the spring of the year, during the decade of the 'sixties, when this graduate of the Boston Latin School joined a minstrel troupe which was being organized in Boston.  Gifted with a good tenor voice and with a fair musical education, he had little trouble in getting a position as a ballad singer at twenty dollars a week.  After a few rehearsals, the company embarked for Rockland, Maine, by steamer. Because the show had not been properly advertised in advance, the troupe withdrew to Thomaston, a village four miles away.  In a parade, the company rode down the village street in a large wagon furnished by the owner of the local hotel, and a crowd assembled in the town hall to witness the début of the burnt cork artists.  After two performances to

[74] The printing included large colored posters, full sheet "cuts," "date slips" announcing the time and place of the performance, great streamers and programs.  The advertising agent, or "advance agent" always preceded the company by a week or two, and in addition to his advertising duties, arranged for licenses, halls, and hotels.

fair-sized houses, the company returned to Rockland, on Penobscot Bay.

At the Atlantic Hall, secured at an expense of eighteen dollars for one night with five dollars for a license, the troupers tried their first engagement in a sizable town of ten thousand. A heavy rainstorm cut down the attendance disastrously, and the company departed for Camden farther up the bay. Although the rental of the theatre here was only four dollars, the minstrels hardly made expenses. The next night found the troupe at the American House in Belfast, whence they proceeded to Searsport. Stockton came next. The Masonic Hall was engaged for three dollars; the audience yielded twelve. At Frankfort Marsh, the company met with its first real encouragement since leaving Boston, for the hall was crowded. Thence, the route proceeded over Winterport to Oldtown. At the latter, a mere backwoods town, an effort was made by the unruly natives to rush the door, the show had to be abandoned, and at the rehearsal the following morning, the company was forced into a fight with a half dozen ruffians of the town who had imbibed too freely of New England rum. A kerosene chandelier was demolished in the scuffle before the interlocutor succeeded in disarming the ringleader of the gang, who was flourishing a huge pistol. Fearful for the safety of the entire troupe when the mill workers of the community should return from work in the evening, a justice of the peace supplied each member of the company with huge navy revolvers and swore them in as a *posse comitatus.*

After a short stop at Orono, the minstrels reached Bangor, then a city of over twenty thousand inhabitants. Its largest hall, seating two thousand, was available for twenty-five dollars a night and a ten dollar license fee. After two profitable performances, the company traveled to Bucksport. Here the manager suggested a reduction in salaries due to poor business, with the result that four members of the company promptly departed for Boston. The others accepted the reduction and the show proceeded through Orland, Ellsworth Falls and Ellsworth to Franklin, traveling by stage part of the way at three or four miles an hour. Then the company proceeded to Cherryfield and Camden, where at long last, in spite of the rainy season, the actors played to a capacity house. With drenched clothing, the troupers arrived at Clare's Hotel in Machias, a county seat and the center of a flourishing lumber region. The town hall was lighted with gas and full of appreciative listeners. "The change from adversity to comfort," wrote the minstrel chronicler, "imparted a glow to the spirits of the boys, and consequently the music was rendered in a joyous manner, and all the acts and jokes participated in with an *elan* that surprised even themselves." The following Tuesday saw the company on its way to Pembroke, an important iron-working district. At Eastport, the last of the American towns before entering the maritime region of Canada, business was not so encouraging.

The company set foot on foreign soil for the first time at Campobello, a little island some three miles from Eastport. The border was aflame at the time with the excitement of the Fenian raids, the foolhardy attempts of Irish-Americans shortly after the close of the Civil War to win freedom for Ireland by twisting the tail of the British lion in Canada. At a number of places along the Canadian-United States frontier, armed bands of Fenians had invaded Canada. Unfortunately, the bass player of the little minstrel company had his huge instrument in a bright green covering. The islanders greeted the American troubadours with sullen silence and deep suspicion, and presently it was discovered that the natives had been expecting a Fenian attack almost daily. The sudden landing of a troupe with a huge green cloth, easily confused with a Fenian banner, caused much excitement. But after mutual explanations, the kindly islanders invited the visiting minstrels to give their entertainment in the military armory. The audience was large and appreciative, and after the show, the hall was cleared for a dance.

The company reëmbarked after these happy experiences, with the minstrel band playing "Auld Lang Syne" and "God Save the Queen."

From Eastport the minstrels traveled by steamer to Saint John, New Brunswick. Here since the two theatres of the town were occupied by a company from Boston and by an amateur minstrel troupe, the professionals decided to continue their journey to the village of Sussex, where a performance was given at Temperance Hall. At Monckton, business was so good that the company ventured to try its fortunes again in Saint John. The first night's show yielded $59.41, the second about $36. By river, the company proceeded to Fredericton, capital of the province. Here terrific rains were encountered, and the manager found it impossible to pay his bills. Consequently baggage and musical instruments were attached by the officers of the law, and the company was permitted to proceed only after considerable difficulty. Returning to Saint John by boat, the organization made one more effort to replenish its empty treasury by hiring the finest hall in Carleton and advertising the show very thoroughly. When these performances also barely met expenses, the company dissolved.

Five of the most courageous members of the troupe, a violinist, 'cellist, cornet player, and two performers, resolved to continue the tour, in the hope

that a company of five might succeed where a larger
organization had proved too much of a financial
burden.   Each of the five remaining troubadours
contributed ten dollars to pay for new posters, pro-
grammes and "dodgers."   The first violin player led
the chorus with voice and instrument; the 'cellist
was a good bass singer; the tenor learned to "double" on the tambourine, and played ends with another member of the troupe who sang comic songs,
baritone in the chorus, and performed on the bones.
A tambourine was constructed out of a fig box and a
leather apron.   By judicious "doubling," the little
company managed to present both a first and second
part.   On the steamer *Empress* they embarked for
Windsor, Nova Scotia, expecting to make their
début in Temperance Hall.   In the absence of
"streamers" to announce the arrival of the show,
the company used bundles of cheap wall-paper,
painted on the reverse side with black and red colors.
Advertisements carrying the inscription, "Go and
See, This Night, the Most Wonderful Combination
of the 19th Century," were posted on the fences.

After a rather discouraging beginning at Windsor, the little troupe moved on to Hantsport, and
thence to Wolfville.   Delighted by a crowded house
which yielded each member eighteen dollars after
all expenses had been paid, the company travelled in
high spirits to Canning, and into the lovely Annap-

olis Valley. At Berwick, a hall was procured for two dollars, and again the company played to a profitable house. At Margaretville, the troupers were able to light their hall with oil lamps graciously furnished by the fishermen and lighthouse keepers in the harbor. The audience proved to be extraordinarily appreciative; few had ever seen a minstrel show before. At Wilmot, Bridgetown, Digby, Weymouth, Lawrencetown, and Annapolis, the old capital of Nova Scotia, business continued to be fairly good and expenses low. The journey to all these towns was made by horse and wagon. At Montangen, a little village inhabited almost exclusively by French Canadians, the ingenious minstrels attracted a crowd by the poster, *"Avis! L'Africaine Chanson et Comedie dans maison école, au soit, a huit heures."* Unfortunately, the notice failed to indicate the necessity of buying tickets of admission. The schoolhouse was filled with French *habitants* in holiday attire, but it proved exceedingly difficult to persuade them to pay for their entertainment. Finally, a member of the company passed his hat among the crowd and by this means managed to collect fifteen dollars. The show proceeded, apparently to the great enjoyment of the audience, although very few could understand a word said or sung.

At Yarmouth, the company found a fine, well-lighted hall, seating fifteen hundred. It was rented for ten dollars a night, and the minstrels played to two capacity houses. There followed stops at Hebron, Tusket, Pubinco, and Barrington Head. At Port Latour the company performed in a fish house, far out on the beach, and collected sixty-five dollars. After numerous stops, the troupe reached Halifax. They did not risk a performance in so large a town, however, with a British garrison and many sailors from British ships in evidence. At the Mount Uniacke Gold Mines the show was given in the schoolhouse, and at Shubenacaddie in a government drill shed. Other visits were made in the coal mining towns of Nova Scotia, and in larger towns like New Glasgow, Pictou, Antigonish, and Sherbrooke. The company then proceeded by easy stages to Cape Breton Island. Here they encountered very active hostility to "Yankees," and unpleasant consequences were avoided only by the timely arrival of some forty Yankee fishermen from two Gloucester schooners which had just put into port. This experience was not typical, however, and all through Nova Scotia the company was well received and financially successful.

At Amherst, the company stayed two nights; in the college town of Sackville they played to a "very distinguished-looking audience," although some of the professors and their ladies apparently were greatly startled by their first experience with an American Negro minstrel performance. After going over the Nova Scotia route a second time in a stage coach drawn by three horses, the company concluded its tour at Halifax. The horses were sold and the minstrels returned to Boston, "with more money in our pockets than when we left."

The trend toward "bigger and better" minstrelsy set in with a vengeance in the late 'seventies and during the 'eighties, with the result that the traditional minstrel show, modified rapidly in almost every detail, was transformed into a burlesque or variety bill. In 1880, Haverly's Mastodons, a company of a hundred members with elaborate stage settings, played in many cities of the United States before touring Germany and England. "Colonel" Haverly, content a few years earlier with a company of "Forty, Count 'em, Forty," now could be satisfied only by a show carrying a hundred performers. In 1881, Leavitt's Gigantean Minstrels set out to conquer the minstrel field. In its organization were many old-time minstrel favorites, like Emmett, Dave Reed, Sam Sanford, Archie Hughes, Frank Moran and Cool Burgess. In the same year, two of Leavitt's companies staged a double street parade in Buffalo, with ninety men and two bands in the procession, and with the old-time stars riding in six car-

riages in the middle of the parade.[75]  Hooley's
Megatherians and Cleveland's Colossals were other
well-known organizations of this type; but the Billy
Sweatnam, Billy Rice and Barney Fagan Minstrels,
in the late 1880's, set the pace in the minstrel world
with a company of one hundred and ten members,
two bands of fourteen musicians each, a sextette of
saxophone players, two drum corps of eight each,
two drum majors and a quartette of mounted
buglers.  During the season of 1882-1883, there
were at least thirty-two minstrel companies on the
road, most of them large and pretentious organizations.[76]  When Haverly's Mastodon Minstrels
played at the Drury Lane Theatre in London in
1884, there were at least sixty visible performers in
the show, eighteen end men with tambourines and
bones, and six star end men who were presented to
the audience in relays.  Needless to add, there was
less and less evidence of genuine Negro characterizations in these elaborate spectacles.  They were

[75] Leavitt, *op. cit.*, pp. 414-416.

[76] Rice, *Monarchs of Minstrelsy*, p. 188.  The list of companies
during the Civil War period and in the two decades after the war is
extremely long.  Among the best known might be mentioned Kim-
berly's Campbells; Rayner's Serenaders; Perham's Burlesque Troupe;
Pierce and Rayner's Christy's; Burgess, Prendergast, Hughes and
Donniker Minstrels; Burgess and LaRue's Minstrels; Booton, Pettengill and Mudge's Minstrels; Trimble's Varieties; Great Arlington
Minstrels; Byington's Minstrels; Hart, Ryman and Barney's Minstrels, and Welch, Hughes and White Minstrels.

vaudeville or variety bills but hardly the blackface art of the 'thirties and 'forties.[77]

In the middle of the 'eighties, the famous minstrel team of McIntyre and Heath became popular, although both performers had been on the stage for some years earlier. Thatcher, Primrose and West's Minstrels, one of the greatest companies in the history of minstrelsy, were playing at the Cincinnati Grand Opera House in December, 1885. The press agent announced that "from the staid merchant who never smiles down to the merry errand-boy who hums minstrel airs when he isn't whistling them, all were anxiously awaiting the coming of this famous troupe." It contained such stars as Billy Rice, one of the greatest end men of all time, whose "gags" were generally new, and singers like Chauncey Olcott, Banks Winter, and Master J. Witmark, the boy soprano. The olio consisted of clog dancing, acrobatic acts, trained dogs, and an afterpiece burlesque on the light opera, the *Mikado*.[78] The California Minstrels, a company of twenty-five performers, played at Havlin's theatre in May, the price of seats ranging from ten to twenty-five cents. Walter Wentworth, "The Red Man from Bagdad," was featured as a contortionist.[79] Two months earlier, Haverly's United American-European Minstrels had

[77] *The Saturday Review*, LVII, 740.
[78] *The Cincinnati Enquirer*, December 6, 1885.
[79] *Ibid.*, May 31, 1885.

made their triumphant entry at Heuck's New Opera
House, with forty-seven performers and most elaborate staging. The finale of the first part represented a banquet scene at the Liverpool Club. In the
olio, the maneuvers of the famous Black Watch regiment were depicted, together with a drill and sword
combat in the Soudan Pass. This was followed
first, by a mammoth song and dance act, "Away
Down in Dixie," and then by a "black visaged
melodrama," "London Lights," described as "pe-
dantic, salamantic, romantic," and "bristling with
burlesque."[80]

In 1886 the Al G. Field Minstrels, one of the last
of the great minstrel organizations, was launched.
In the fall of 1887, McNish, Johnson and Slavin's
Minstrels and The Gorman's Spectacular Minstrels
visited the Chicago Opera House. The former
featured a first part with a setting which represented the White House Lawn Serenade; the latter
stressed "The Siamese Twins! The Hindoo Ballet
Dancers! The Trick Elephants! The Chinese Giants!
The Headless Man!" as "the new era in minstrelsy"
and "the climax of minstrel greatness." The performance apparently was quite mediocre, and the
number of songs rendered in falsetto, "the style of
emasculated vocalism . . . especially pleasing to

[80] *The Cincinnati Enquirer*, March 22, 1885.

minstrel audiences," was larger than usual.[81] Sweatnam, Billy Rice, and Barney Fagan's Progressive Minstrels coming to Chicago in the same season, appeared at Hooley's Theatre in a program including a military musical festival, Apollo Belvideres, and Liberty Enlightening the World. The orchestra of seventeen was attired in the uniform of the French guard, the twelve vocalists of the company in the court dress of the period of King George II, while the comedians appeared in the garb of American soldiers. Sweatnam and Rice presented a new sketch entitled "Oratory." When Haverly's Mastodon Minstrels opened at the Columbia Theatre they featured "the superb vocal choir" at admission charges from twenty-five cents to a dollar.[82]

In 1887, the Thatcher, Primrose and West organization was performing at Niblo's Garden, the Harlem Theatre, and the Grand Opera House in New York City. Thatcher appeared in monologues, and the program concluded with a burlesque on grand opera, which introduced, among other things, "a highly moral and excruciatingly funny ballet."[83] Two years later, Primrose and West's Millionaire Minstrels reached the climax of expensive and gorgeous first parts in their performances at the Grand

[81] *The Chicago Tribune,* December 4, 5, 6, 1887; September 11, 1887.

[82] *Ibid.,* September 25, October 2, 1887.

[83] *New York Times,* January 11, February 22, December 11, 1887.

Opera House in Philadelphia. The show featured a "crystal first part" with twin drum majors, the programme being the usual hodge-podge to be expected by this time of all minstrel organizations. Primrose appeared as an English swell, and participated in a burlesque entitled "Cremation," a clever take-off of one of the most popular illusions featured at the time by Herman, the great magician. The act was silly enough in itself. Bob Slavin, one of the comedians, suffered himself to be led to a peculiar crematory for the promise of four dollars. A fire then was started under the three-hundred-dollar-a-week comedian, while West and another funmaker provided the merriment while looking for the ashes of their cremated friend. The act ended with Slavin appearing in the parquet of the theatre. The olio contained a bicycle trick rider, a sixteen foot somersault from bar to bar, a musical act, and the march of the "popinjays" in which the performers appeared in red and yellow satin suits, with monocles and walking sticks. West served as interlocutor.[84]

Carncross' Minstrels also appeared in Philadelphia in 1889, featuring the travesty, "McGinty in Town," and introducing the famous song, "Down Went McGinty."[85] At the Eleventh Street Opera House, famous in the history of minstrelsy for its

[84] *Philadelphia Press,* September 22, 24, 29, 1889.
[85] *Ibid.,* December 15, 1889.

many years of minstrel stock companies, Frank Dumont was presenting one burlesque on the corrupt
city administration of Philadelphia and another on
the popular craze for bicycle clubs.[86]  W. S. Cleveland's Minstrels, a company of over forty, advertised a $20,000 first part, "Venetian Nights," at the
Philadelphia Central Theatre during the fall of
1889.  In addition, they presented "an Amazing
Antipodean Annex, Sugimotos, Royal Imperial Japanese, Bright Tiny Little All-Rights," which apparently was the minstrel way of advertising nothing
more exciting than a troupe of Japanese jugglers and
acrobats.  Willis P. Sweatnam and Billy Rice were
the black-face stars with this company.[87]  Other organizations visiting Philadelphia during 1889 were
the San Francisco Minstrels, the Gormans, and
Cushman and Thomas' Ideal Minstrels.[88]

In 1896, not an especially prosperous year, since
the country had not recovered fully from the panic
of 1893, Bourman and Young's High Class Minstrels, with nineteen performers and a band of fourteen musicians, toured Oregon and Montana in their
own sleeping and dining cars, and played to large
audiences.[89]  In the same year, the Plantation Minstrels and Wonder Cornet Band, a small company

[86] *Philadelphia Press*, October 1, 1889.
[87] *Ibid.*, October 13, 1889.
[88] *Ibid.*, November 17, December 1, 22, 1889.
[89] *The New York Clipper*, March 14, 1896.

of eleven consisting of two end men, three balladists, a baton juggler, three comedians and dancers, and the leader of the band and orchestra, in which apparently all of the company "doubled" on various instruments, were finishing their twenty-sixth week in Minnesota. Al G. Field was reporting good business in Ohio and Pennsylvania towns in spite of blizzards and the Lenten season.[90] The Field company had just concluded a successful tour of Canada, although blizzards and deep snow had made street parades impossible, and the owner was planning a big burlesque with six specialty acts for the following season.[91] The J. H. Haverly American-European Minstrels opened a new season on August 1, 1896, with a company of fifty and two special railroad cars,[92] although Haverly's Mastodon Minstrels had closed prematurely early in the year at New Orleans, because the company would not accept a reduction in salaries induced by extraordinarily poor business in the South.[93]

*The New York Clipper* for January 4, 1896, listed ten minstrel companies which were touring various parts of the United States from Texas to North Dakota and from Massachusetts to Kansas. Fifteen years later the list had been greatly reduced,

[90] *The New York Clipper*, March 21, 1896.
[91] *Ibid.*, March 7, 1896.
[92] *Ibid.*, May 30, 1896.
[93] *Ibid.*, February 8, 1896.

until in April, 1919, Al G. Field declared that there
were but three first class minstrel organizations
playing in the United States, although other companies of inferior grade and fewer performers still
were appearing in some parts of the country.

The days of the American minstrel show, except
as a vehicle for amateurs, seemed over.  The end,
which might have been forecast at least as early as
the 1880's, did not actually come until the second
decade of the twentieth century.  Burnt cork performers, of course, are still very popular on the
vaudeville stage, over the radio, and in musical comedies.  But when the Al G. Field Minstrels, with its
record of a continuous existence since 1886, closed
rather suddenly in Cincinnati in the spring of 1928,
seven years after the death of its distinguished
owner and manager, it may be said that the final
curtain was rung down on what, at one time, was
America's most successful form of entertainment.
The distinctive contribution of the American theatre
to the history of the stage had been made.  In 1924
the passing of Lew Dockstader, one of the greatest
of the minstrel stars of all time, like that of Field
three years earlier, was "the symbol of the death of
an American institution."  Still earlier, in 1911, the
final curtain had been rung down at the Eleventh
Street Opera House in Philadelphia, the oldest theatre in the country devoted to minstrelsy, and used

almost exclusively for this form of entertainment
since 1855. The old structure, made famous by such
stars as Carncross, Sanford, Frank Dumont, and
Weber and Fields, had to make way for the demands
of big business and the curtain came down on May
13 to the tune of "Auld Lang Syne," after a special
evening devoted to the old-time minstrel songs.[94]
The reign of the "mammoth," "original," "superb,"
"refined," "gigantean," "mastodon" minstrel companies on the American professional stage had come
to a close, and there are few signs on the theatrical
horizon that would lead even the most optimistic to
predict a revival of this peculiarly American form
of entertainment.

Much might be written in an effort to explain the
passing of this American institution. One historian
of the American theatre has dismissed the subject
with the statement that minstrelsy was "an art that
was to endure for as many decades as the artless
disposition of our countrymen could permit."[95] But
this explanation does not take into account many
specific changes in the minstrel profession which
were important contributing causes for the decline
of the burnt cork entertainments.

In the first place, it is necessary to point out that
minstrel performances became financially unprofitable for a variety of reasons, and that they felt

[94] *The New York Clipper*, May 27, 1911.
[95] Odell, *op. cit.*, IV, 674.

keenly the ruthless operation of the law of competition which affected the theatrical as well as other
fields of business enterprise. Minstrel shows became financially unprofitable not only because of the
competition of other forms of amusement which
were supplanting them in the popular taste, but also
because of the rapidly rising expense of theatrical
productions, the cost of stage settings, advertising,
equipment of various sorts, and salaries. It proved
impossible to raise the admission charges from the
customary twenty-five and fifty cents sufficiently to
meet these increased costs of production. Patrons
of the theatre hesitated to pay two or three dollars
for a main floor seat when other kinds of entertainment were available at fifty or seventy-five cents.
This was especially true when the moving picture
theatres began to provide dramatic though inanimate
entertainment at these prices. Many present day
theatrical managers are seriously considering how
the extremes between these two sets of seat prices
may be narrowed. All kinds of suggestions, including
proposals to build larger theatres, to restore the old-
fashioned gallery, and to install amplifiers for the
more remote seats, have been seriously made. An attempt by the minstrels, as in the case of other dramatic companies, to curtail expenses and to live
within the revenue coming in at the box office, usually
meant still greater losses in patronage, because of the

competition of other forms of entertainment and the public's dislike for "cheap" performances. The recent syndicating of the theatre and amusement business hardly applied to the minstrel shows because the latter already were declining rapidly when "captains of industry" began applying their methods to the theatrical field. In the struggle for the survival of the fittest, Negro minstrelsy had to participate, but under very unfavorable conditions and with comparatively little chance of success.

Charley White's Minstrels played at the old Bowery Theatre in 1854 to an audience that could get two parquet seat tickets for twenty-five cents. At another theatre in New York, tickets selling for the same price, carried a refreshment coupon good for either a drink or a cigar.[96] In some places, tickets were to be had for as little as ten cents. These prices seem to have been standard for the first two decades when minstrelsy flourished. Few theatre-goers at that time dreamed of a day when they would have to pay more than twenty-five cents for a seat, for minstrel magnates were making money at these prices.[97] The balance sheet of Christy's Minstrels, reprinted in Davidge's *Footlight Flashes*, shows rising profits, even at these low admission rates. The annual surplus earned by this organization steadily

[96] Brown, *History of the New York Stage,* I, 361; *The New York Clipper,* November 20, 1858.
[97] Brown, *History of the American Stage,* p. 174.

mounted from $294.92 in 1842 to $26,465.50 in
1850, and the total surplus for the twelve years ending in 1854 was $181,087.[98] But the same table
shows rapidly mounting expenditures also. In 1842,
for a season of sixty-nine performances, the costs of
production amounted to $1,652.60; by 1854, for
two hundred and two performances, they reached
$39,338.98.

Salaries ranged from six to twelve dollars a
week for the average performer during most of the
'fifties.[99] M. B. Leavitt, prominent in the theatrical
world for half a century as a manager and producer,
is authority for the statement that Dan Bryant retired from the minstrel stage with a fortune of seventy-five thousand dollars, Neil Bryant with fifty
thousand dollars, and that other noted managers and
performers, like Duprez, Morris, Sharpley, and
Brower also left substantial estates. George Christy's
income was estimated at twelve thousand dollars a
year. Stars like Eph Horn, in their prime, could expect salaries from $100 to $125 a week. This, however, was exceptional and applied only to star performers of the first magnitude. The ordinary "star"
might receive from $40 to $75 a week in the period
from 1870 to 1885, a good basso was paid $15 to $30
a week, the leading violin player $25 to $40, end men

[98] P. 128.
[99] Brown, *History of the New York Stage*, I, 362.

and comedians from $15 to $40, and the ordinary
musician from $10 to $25 a week. To these figures
transportation and hotel bills must be added in most
cases.

To organize and launch a first class minstrel
company on the road in the late 1860's required a
salary roll of approximately four hundred dollars a
week for eighteen performers. It is safe to estimate
that twice that amount was necessary to finance the
same kind of company in the next decade. Of course
less expensive companies could be organized for
shows in the smaller towns and in rural sections. In
the early 'seventies, a show frankly intended for the
"provinces" probably involved an expenditure for
salaries of not more than $250 a week. The two
end men might receive as much as twenty-five dollars a week and expenses; the interlocutor twenty, a
falsetto soprano fifteen, the falsetto alto or baritone
singer twelve, and the tenor fifteen. The first violin
in the orchestra would probably get as much as the
end men, the second violin fifteen dollars a week, the
first cornet fifteen, the second cornet twelve, the flute
or clarinet twelve, and the double bass twelve. A
clog dancer could be obtained for this type of show
at twelve dollars a week, and a good advance agent
might receive twenty dollars or more.[100]

By the 1880's and 1890's, the weekly cost had

[100] *Negro Minstrelsy, the Old Fashioned Troupes* (Boston, 189-).

risen to fifteen hundred dollars plus hotel expenses for the better shows; and by 1912, leading companies of similar size and talent had salary budgets of about twenty-five hundred dollars a week.[101]   Advertisements designed to attract talent into the profession announced in 1880 that a minstrel performer might expect from twenty-five to a hundred dollars a week, provided he would supply his own wardrobe and meet the expense of arranging his songs for the orchestra.[102]   The noted actor, Francis Wilson, began his career at five dollars a week with Sam S. Sanford's minstrel troupe; but before he abandoned the burnt cork circle for the drama, he was receiving one hundred and fifty dollars a week as a member of the minstrel team, Mackin and Wilson.[103]   In 1871, Hart, Ryan and Barney's Minstrels advertised a new company, featuring an English quartette at "four hundred dollars in gold each week."[104]

During the last three decades of minstrelsy, salaries, which once ranged from thirty to seventy-five dollars a week even for star performers, trebled and quadrupled. Stagehands demanded seventy-five dollars a week, instead of twenty-five as formerly, and labor unions insisted on the employment of three or four men back stage where one had sufficed. A large

---

[101] Leavitt, *op. cit.*, pp. 37-38.

[102] Edward James, *The Amateur Negro Minstrel Guide* (New York, 1880), p. 14.

[103] *Francis Wilson's Life of Himself* (New York, 1924), pp. 36-45.

[104] *The New York Clipper*, May 27, 1871.

organization like the Field Minstrels in recent years carried a carpenter, a chief electrician, an assistant electrician, a property man and a fly man. The latter, whose chief business it was to be up in the fly galleries to pull ropes at the proper time, received a salary of eighty dollars a week, plus transportation. It was a minstrel manager who wrote, "When I look at the salary list these days, I'm more than half persuaded that the real stage stars are the property men, grips, flymen, and stage carpenters."[105]

The star balladist of the Field company, an excellent high baritone, received four hundred and seventy-five dollars a week, the leading comedian and black face performer four hundred dollars, and another first class tenor received two hundred and fifty dollars a week. There was not a member in the company who was paid less than sixty dollars a week, plus transportation, hotel charges, and wardrobe. The Al G. Field Minstrels often spent ten thousand dollars for the show's wardrobe for one season with scenery costing several thousand. To this must be added the cost of other stage properties, electrical devices, a band of musicians who received union salaries, railroad charges for hauling and parking two special cars, advertising, the salary of two advance agents, and the percentage charges by theatres in which the company performed.

[105] *The Billboard*, September 7, 1929, p. 49.

It was almost impossible to charge prices of admission high enough to meet these enormous expenses. Minstrel shows retained their drawing power longest in the Southern states, but unfortunately the theatres in many of the small towns where the minstrel craze has persisted even to the present day were too small to make the bookings pay. It became increasingly difficult on the other hand to secure the necessary consecutive bookings in the larger cities by which the long and expensive jumps from place to place could be avoided. Show houses were being bought up by the moving picture interests, which presented cheap competition which minstrelsy could not meet. In the light of these circumstances, and in view of the higher salaries by which vaudeville, burlesques and musical comedies lured the stars of the minstrel field to a new and increasingly popular type of entertainment, it is easy to sympathize with the complaints of minstrel managers and realize that financial considerations were of first importance in the decline of minstrelsy.

But this economic interpretation is not the only explanation for the disappearance of the professional minstrel show, and various other causes have been suggested to account for the great slump in box office receipts. Some have found the explanation for the decline of minstrelsy in the degeneration of the minstrel show itself. Protests against the "nui-

sance and the slang of the so-called 'Negro minstrelsy,'" and against the impropriety of certain
features of minstrel performances can be found in
great numbers, beginning at least as early as the
1860's. A Southern slave-holder who wrote on
Negro minstrelsy complained as early as 1855 that
in a whole volume of minstrel songs which he had
examined, he could find "only ten with any trace
of genuineness."[106] In Boston, minstrelsy began to
decline as an amusement fit for the better classes
before 1860.[107] Critic after critic complained that
"The old-time Negro character has been sunk out of
sight and the vulgarity of the game has taken the
place of the innocent comicalities that were in vogue
forty years ago." Such criticisms usually were accompanied by more or less severe denunciation of
the immorality, the improvidence, the love for gaudy
display and other alleged vices of these "gangs of
nigger singers."[108] Whether these criticisms would
apply to the better type of minstrel productions may
be seriously questioned, however.

Most of the criticism centered on the complaint
that the minstrels did not remain in their special

[106] *Putnam's Monthly*, V, 72-79, January, 1855.

[107] See H. A. Clapp, *Reminiscences of a Dramatic Critic* (Boston,
1902) ; John J. Jennings, *op. cit.;* and Charles Mackay, *Life and Liberty in America, or Sketches of a Tour in the United States and
Canada in 1857-8* (New York, 1859).

[108] Jennings, *op. cit.*, p. 371.

field as delineators of Negro character but only too
often deserted their genial task of imitating humor-
ously and sympathetically the darky population of
the country. Minstrel programs were cluttered up
with such utterly incongruous acts as sentimental
Irish ballads, silly "Dutch" comedy of the slap-stick
variety, and the variety features of the olio. Even
the first part frequently was put on in Oriental
splendor and with an ever-growing personnel, a far
cry from the simple imitations of the early black
face actors.[109] At best, Negro minstrelsy always
was more of a burlesque than a sincere and truthful
imitation of Negro life; consequently, as the "musical and picturesque extravagance" of minstrelsy
developed, its significance as a distinctively American stage institution proportionally declined.[110]
There was an ever-widening gap between the mimicry of pre-Civil War days, with its typical, simple
Negro songs and dances, and the "Punch and Judy
costumes," "stale newspaper jokes," and "mere fool-
ish and unmeaning cackle" of later years.[111] Caricaturing supplanted carefully studied plantation
types, and sentimental ballads of every description,
parodies, and clog dances drove from the program
such themes and melodies as Emmett's "Old Dan

[109] Brander Matthews, *loc. cit.,* p. 758.
[110] See Quinn, *op. cit.,* p. 335.
[111] Leavitt, *op. cit.,* p. 38.

Tucker," while coarse comedy replaced the whimsical humor of old Negro types.[112]

These criticisms concerning the disintegration and deterioration of minstrel programs were loudly made in some quarters even before 1860. *The Clipper,* in 1857, contrasted Bryant's Minstrels with the "new-fangled notions which some troupes attempt to palm off upon us as Negro eccentricities," and observed, "while . . . other companies are making higher flights of fancy in the regions of darkness, and are slowly taking leave of those old style entertainments in the black art, it is gratifying to find that we have yet among us those who will not suffer the original type of Negro eccentricity to die out altogether." "The connecting link between the days of minstrelsy of old, and those of the present time," the critic continued, "are the Bryant Minstrels." This troupe seems to have excelled for years in its clever delineations of the old plantation Negro, as well as of the more uncommon dandy Negroes of

[112] See a letter by Sam S. Sanford in *The New York Clipper,* May 28, 1871. The same sentiment was expressed by an old advance agent of minstrel shows in the 'seventies as follows, "The time was when the black faced troubadour sang the pensive melodies of Stephen Foster, or all hands united in a stirring walk-a-round of Emmett, as is the wont of the plantation darkie in festive times. Nowadays the end man ditties a catch from a London music dive, and in the olio, instead of negro life as found way down South, we have a few city barbers and devotèes of 4-11-44 pictured for our edification. The *prima donna* aspires to be a Nilsson, the *prima tenore* thinks himself a Brignoli, and to satisfy their ambition we have burlesque opera." Charles H. Day, *op. cit.,* p. 11.

more northerly latitudes. Certainly Dan Bryant's presentation of the original 'Essence of Old Virginny' was comparable only with Daddy Rice's 'Jim Crow' as a classic of America Negro minstrelsy. But burnt cork artists of the Bryant type seemed to be fighting a losing battle. In the words of an old trouper, who in 1929, in his retirement, discussed the decline of his profession, "the Southern atmosphere got lost. It gave way to the mixing of chorus girls in the show, and minstrelsy became musical comedy, 'corked up,' and billed as minstrelsy." The only original feature left of the old-time show was the street parade.[113]

In a very recent treatment of minstrelsy in the United States, the authors, who are entirely sympathetic with the minstrel performers and. sigh for a revival of this American institution, suggest that "when the settings began to look like a Drury Lane pantomime and the men dressed like gorgeous courtiers in a magnificent kingdom, not to speak of the increasing tendency to substitute white faces for black, the minstrel show began to lose some of its distinctive flavour." The same writers believe that "left to itself, with its individual technique and its familiar formulas of wit and sentiment, all based upon homely realities of human experience, the min-

[113] For these and similar opinions, see *The New York Clipper*, September 12, 1857; December 26, 1857; December 31, 1859; and *The Billboard*, April 6, 1929.

strel show might easily have survived, and under similar conditions it might even live again. . . ."[114]

Whatever the future may hold for minstrelsy in these days of a really astounding revival of interest in Negro music, dancing, and folklore, at least one successful manager, the late Al G. Field, refuted this attack on the moderns by pointing out that for one season he actually staged "a simon-pure, old-time minstrel show" with the best talent available and with appropriate costumes, and yet the season turned out to be the least profitable in many years. Indeed, the experiment was so disastrous that Field had to change his show in the middle of the season, going back to blackface comedians, white-face singers, and the other more modern features of minstrelsy.[115] "Lassus" White, one of the best of the modern blackface performers appearing on the vaudeville stage in minstrel sketches, has made a special effort to depict the real Negro of the South. But he has found it difficult to get Northern audiences, unfamiliar with the Southern Negro type, to appreciate fully his real darky humor and his excellent delineations.

Another fact to be emphasized in this connection is that the minstrel show was a wholly masculine affair. It therefore had no "sex appeal" or sex fascination for its audiences, and when competition appeared in the form of the musical comedies, the

[114] Paskman and Spaeth, *op. cit.*, p. 239.
[115] Al G. Field, *Watch Yourself Go By* (Columbus, 1912), p. 521.

variety bills, and the movie "thrillers," where this important element in human experience is never overlooked, minstrelsy could not withstand the competition. Minstrelsy, "a simple and unsophisticated entertainment," could not hope to hold its own against the "girl shows" of modern times. Its program seemed sadly limited and monotonous, in comparison with these new forms of entertainment.

As vaudeville salaries and musical comedy salaries attracted the best minstrel men, the public followed its favorites into these new lines, and minstrel patronage declined. With decreasing receipts, minstrel managers found it impossible to battle their new competitors on anything like equal terms. Good artists could always get more money and have less work to do in burlesques and vaudeville acts. Finally, the amateur craze for minstrel performances, based on the false assumption that any group can produce a minstrel program, undoubtedly helped to kill minstrelsy as a professional form of amusement.

The competition of the moving pictures cut still more deeply into the minstrel business. Every little town and village, for which the arrival of a traveling minstrel show once was the event of the theatrical season, now has its movie house, running perhaps continuously from noon to midnight each day, perhaps open at least three or four nights a week, and always at prices low enough to enable enthusiastic patrons to go with their families several times a week. How the decline in minstrelsy during the last generation compares with a similar decline in the number of grand opera and Shakespeare companies, or with the number of circuses on tour, would be an interesting question to study.

Today, minstrelsy is the chief indoor sport of amateurs. It is a leading source of revenue for the "benefits" of all kinds of organizations with mortgages to liquidate or other funds to raise, from Ladies of the Mystic Shrine, Kiwanis Clubs and Elks to policemen's and firemen's mutual insurance and protective associations. Numerous volumes have appeared in recent years, dealing with the production of amateur minstrel shows, and containing complete first parts and specialties, eloquent testimony to the steady demand of amateurs for guidance in the fundamentals of the blackface art.[116] Many former stars of the professional stage now make a living by developing and directing home-talent amateur productions. One minstrel show producer in one season

---

[116] See for example, Herbert Preston Powell, *The World's Best Book of Minstrelsy* (Philadelphia, 1926); also the advertisements in almost any recent number of *The Billboard*. Older manuals are Jack Haverly, *Negro Minstrels* (Chicago, 1902); William Courtright, *The Complete Minstrel Guide* (Chicago, 1901); W. B. Dick, *Dick's Ethiopian Scenes, Variety Sketches and Stump Speeches* (1879), and *Dick's Stump Speeches and Minstrel Jokes* (1889); *Francis and Day's "Jokelets," as performed by the Mohawk, Moore and Burgess' Minstrels* (n.d.); and Frank Dumont, *Frank Dumont's Minstrel Joke-Book* (1898).

alone organized thirty-two such shows with all local talent, in which over thirty-five hundred performers participated.[117]

On the professional stage, minstrel acts are still popular in vaudeville and variety bills. Indeed, some of the best of the modern minstrel stars, comedians like Bert Swor or "Lassus" White, singers like Jack Richards and Billy Church, as well as little companies like the Dan Fitch Minstrels, are favorites on the Keith-Albee and other vaudeville circuits all over the country. "Lassus" White, for eight years the owner of one of the best of the recent minstrel shows on the road, recently appeared on the Keith-Albee circuit in "The Blackville Polar Expedition," an excellent sketch reminiscent of the best of the old minstrel "after-pieces." Bert Swor, Neil O'Brien, and many others have appeared in the vaudeville houses. A much poorer type of blackface performance is occasionally seen in medicine shows, street fairs, carnivals, and midway attractions. Minstrel methods are introduced in musical comedies, and occasionally the theatre-goer sees a short minstrel first part staged as one scene in a musical extravaganza. The late Bert Williams, one of the comparatively few Negro performers who played in white companies, and burnt cork artists like George Thatcher, McIntyre and Heath, Al Jolson, Frank Tinney and

[117] *The Billboard*, June 8, 1929, p. 37.

Eddie Cantor, have appeared in many musical comedies, as blackface performers, although it will be generally admitted that there is little left of their Negro impersonations except "mammy songs," "shuffles" and "blues."

In 1928, the Schuberts sent out a first class production, called *Headin' South,* with a company of over eighty which included such minstrel headliners as McIntyre and Heath, and Bert Swor, for years the premier comedian with the Field Minstrels. The show featured a minstrel first part, and was in every way a first class organization. Even this excellent company found it difficult to secure profitable consecutive bookings. After playing in a few cities like Wilmington, Philadelphia, Washington, Detroit, Cleveland and a two weeks' run in Chicago, the play was taken off the road in Buffalo and closed after only eight weeks. The owners of the Field Minstrels, although offered bookings for twenty consecutive weeks in the South, recently refused to take the risk of sending a new organization on the road.[118]

All-Negro musical shows have become extraordinarily popular recently, even in the high priced theatres, to say nothing of cheaper burlesque houses. Over the radio, the public has been introduced, often

[118] For a good discussion of the absorption of minstrel methods and technique by farce and musical comedy, see Gaines, *op. cit.,* pp. 104-109. For a vivid impression of the rapid decline in the number of travelling minstrel companies, one need only follow the files of a theatrical magazine like *The New York Clipper.*

in the form of advertising schemes, to some excellent minstrel acts which depend for success wholly on the dialogue and the songs. Famous comedy teams, like Moran and Mack, the "Two Black Crows," received extraordinarily large sums for a series of short minstrel acts presented by microphone over a number of weeks. That the old-time minstrel show seems to fit easily into the limitations of the broadcasting station, is demonstrated by the fact that in 1928, Geoffrey O'Hara, formerly with Dockstader's Minstrels, arranged for the broadcasting, over a great radio network, of songs and jokes assembled from a Dockstader show of twenty years ago. In the Southern states, a number of troupes, most of them composed of colored performers, still present minstrel shows under canvas tents. Their shows generally are of the slap-stick variety. Colored troupes, like Charles Callender's Georgia Colored Minstrels, the company of Hicks and Sawyer, the Booker and Clayton Georgia Minstrels, and others, have enjoyed considerable popularity in the South for many years. Negro companies, it is curious to point out, almost always black up for these minstrel acts.

. Although the day of the old-time minstrel show seems to be definitely over, a surprisingly large number of small organizations with comparatively low salary budgets, continue to hang on to their disappearing clientele with grim determination, either venturing into the provinces or playing short summer engagements. Recently, J. A. Coburn, well-known for many years as a minstrel producer with a dogged determination to cling to the last to a rapidly dying form of entertainment, tried the new experiment of a motorized show which went from town to town in the South by auto bus, carrying the performers and all necessary equipment to each of the theatres where a performance was advertised. A combination of misfortunes, partly connected with minstrelsy and partly with disastrous investments in Florida real estate, soon brought this newest experiment in minstrel shows to an untimely end. When the show disbanded, "Sugarfoot" Williams, one of its premier comedians, performed in various night clubs in the larger cities of the South and then joined a traveling jazz orchestra.

F. S. Wolcott's Rabbit Foot Minstrels opened in June, 1929, under canvas at Port Gibson, Mississippi. This organization carried fifty people, including a twenty-five piece band and "a chorus of twenty high browns," and travelled about in the two special cars, the "Dan Emmett," a sleeping car, and the "Southland," a dining and baggage car, formerly used by the Al G. Field Minstrels. Performances were given in an electrically lighted tent, equipped with a dozen electric fans. J. S. Lincoln's Minstrels, another motorized organization, reported playing to good business in the spring of 1929, in Arkansas and Texas. The Alabama Minstrels were playing in Arkansas also. Other companies, either playing in the South in 1929 or announcing their intention to begin performances during that year, include Miles' Mighty Minstrels; Jordan's Swiftfoot Minstrels, a motorized show reporting a forty-two week schedule of performances; Richards and Pringle's Georgia Minstrels; the Florida Blossoms; Warner and Moorman's Famous Brown Derby Minstrels (playing in the Middle West); the Royer Brothers' Great American Minstrels (which toured the towns of the Middle West by auto, until the show was stranded in Arkansas); John R. Van Arnam's Minstrels, one of the oldest of the smaller shows, which absorbed most of the talent of Coburn and White's organizations when these were taken off the road; and The Southern Minstrels with a personnel of twenty-seven. Frank Kirk, after forty-four years on the stage, spent mostly in minstrels, signed a contract recently to twang tunes on queer instruments and to do grotesque minstrel comedy with Beck and Walker's Minstrels. Jack Linder's Legionnaire Minstrels, originally intended for the RKO vaudeville houses, began a season of forty-two weeks in September, 1929, playing the Erlanger houses. The show, with a company of forty, is really a minstrel vaudeville unit, dealing with the frolics of doughboys during the Great War. The promoters planned to enlist American Legion support in many of the towns visited, in return for a percentage of the box office receipts.

Clay Hubbard's Harmonica Minstrels played during the summer months of 1929 in the resorts of the Catskill Mountains. The Sugarfoot Greene Minstrels were touring the Southern States. Emmett Welch's Minstrels, an organization which is a connecting link with the old Carncross and Dixey company, took to the road in 1929, after Welch's Theatre in Philadelphia was razed to make room for a business structure. For many seasons, the organization had played engagements at the Million Dollar Pier in Atlantic City. The Steel Pier Minstrels are now in their thirtieth season at this famous resort. Ten years ago, twenty-six minstrel companies were on the road.

Here the story of the decline of American minstrel shows might end, were it not for the fact that the "talkies" promise a revival of this venerable art. Probably this new version of minstrelsy will have only a remote resemblance to the performances of the early burnt cork artists. Seven minstrel shows were on the "talkie" programs by May, 1929, and "the twinkle of tambourines and the rhythmic rattle of the bones" are being heard again in Hollywood. Optimists say that "Hollywood has gone minstrel," and the minstrel show has been pronounced ideal for this new form of entertainment. It permits the introduction of many specialties, very little plot is needed, and there is virtually no limit to the "wise cracking" by which the minstrel boys can enliven the film. *Universal* seems to have started the new experiment with "The Minstrel Man," starring Eddie Leonard. Into this film, Leonard took with him two of the old songs with which he was identified in the days when he was on the minstrel stage. In "Ida" and "Roly-Boly Eyes," he first developed that syncopated syllabication style which won him fame in the burnt cork circle. *Fox* followed immediately, signing the venerable team of McIntyre and Heath to a contract, and *Paramount* engaged Moran and Mack, the "Two Black Crows," and Bert Swor, to make a picture called "Why Bring That Up." The *Pathé* company has produced "The Rainbow Man," with a big minstrel first part, and the *Warner* organization has planned "The Minstrel Boy," in which Al Jolson may be featured. There is a proposal to have George Wilson, an eighty-six year old veteran, long retired from the minstrel stage, enter the "talkies" with his famous monolog, "Waltz Me Again," a classic of bygone days.

Evidently the "talkie" producers have been tremendously impressed by the success of their first crop of minstrel pictures, notably such triumphs as

Moran and Mack's "Why Bring That Up," and
Eddie Dowling's "The Rainbow Man," the latter
being a picture which features a star performer who
has never trouped as a minstrel. The play itself is
a veritable glorification of minstrelsy, and depicts
life backstage with a small minstrel company. The
future of minstrelsy seems to lie in the lap of Hollywood.[119]

[119] For current news of the minstrel profession, see *The Billboard*,
which contains each week a special column devoted to minstrelsy.
The issue for September 7, 1929, carried a list of twenty-six
minstrel companies on tour just ten years ago. It includes A. G.
Allen's Big Minstrels, Harry Hunt, manager; Arnold & Quick's
Greater Minstrels, John B. Quick, manager; Beach & Bowers' Fa-
mous Minstrels, Busby's Minstrels, J. A. Coburn's Minstrels, Al G.
Field Minstrels, Fisher & Fleming's American Minstrels, Happy
Harry Foot's Minstrels, Georgia Black and Tan Minstrels, R. M.
Harvey's Greater Minstrels, Joseph C. Herbert's Minstrels, Gus Hill's
Minstrels, F. C. Huntington's Minstrels, Herbert La She's Min-
strels, Lincoln's Alabama Minstrels, Mallory's Original Mobile Min-
strels, Bert Wilson's Moose Minstrels, John F. Murphy's Minstrels
(Steel Pier, Atlantic City), Nashville Students' Minstrels, J. C.
O'Brien's Georgia Minstrels, Neil O'Brien's Great American Min-
strels, Price-Bonelli Greater New York Minstrels, Renix Bros.' Minstrels, Victory Minstrels and F. S. Wolcott's Rabbit-Foot Minstrels.

# CHAPTER IV

## THE TECHNIQUE OF THE AMERICAN MINSTREL SHOW

To some degree at least, the minstrels themselves were responsible for the collapse of their once successful form of entertainment. There was little similarity between the performances of the last two decades of minstrelsy and those of the earlier period. From a simple, and fairly truthful imitation of Negro folkmusic and Negro folkways, as practiced by the pioneers of the burnt cork profession, minstrelsy had developed into a mixture of comic opera, burlesque, variety acts and buffoonery hard to distinguish from other forms of entertainment in which the present-day theatre-going public is interested. This change in the technique of minstrel shows, together with the competition of new forms of amusement, slowly but relentlessly sapped the vitality of minstrelsy as a professional form of theatricals.

At the first performance of the Virginia Minstrels, in 1843, the chairs of the four performers accidentally were arranged in the form of a semicircle, and the costumes designed by Emmett had the big collars and swallow-tail coats which became characteristic of minstrel productions. Apparently, there was no conscious design to set the standards of a new type of performance in this arrangement. Moreover, as Emmett pointed out in later years, all the performers served as endmen and interlocutors; in fact no distinction was made among the various members of the company, and no specialized functions were assigned to any one of them. Every performer participated in the program of songs, dances, "walk arounds," and instrumental music.

The stereotyped form of the American minstrel show, to which it conformed fairly rigidly to the present time, probably had its origin with the E. P. Christy Minstrels. It was Christy who consciously adopted the semi-circular seating arrangement for the "first part," with a middleman at the center, and two endmen, one equipped with a pair of bones or castanets, and the other with a tambourine, sitting at the extremities of the semi-circle. Christy also was the first to harmonize various acts into the standard pattern of a "first part" minstrel performance, with a well-coördinated program of songs and jokes, and lively repartee between the endmen and the middleman. The "first part" was followed by an olio, consisting of a series of variety acts, and in the early years, invariably closing with a farce, or singing and dancing number, in which the entire company participated. As time went on, minstrel performances became more elaborate, the companies increased in size, and the expenditures of managers and owners on stage equipment and scenery became more lavish, but the essential pattern of minstrel shows remained substantially the same.

The curtain rose upon a group of minstrels attired in brilliant costumes, usually some variety of dress suits, "a rainbow of shining darkies," with great collars, striped trousers, and gaudy silks, arranged in a half circle, and with the minstrel band or orchestra either seated in the orchestra pit, or more often, arranged in the rear of the performers on the stage. Sometimes only the band was visible when the curtain rose, and the performers entered from backstage or from the wings. After a lively song, and a more or less elaborate drill back and forth across the stage, in which the endmen usually entered last, the performers always managed to reach their chairs in the circle just as the song came to an end with a special flourish from the musicians. With a final blare from the trumpets, a roll on the drums, or a chord from the full orchestra, the song reached its close, and the interlocutor gave the famous stereotyped command, "Gentlemen, be seated." The show was on.[1]

[1] The Christy Minstrels at one time used the following song, entitled "Down the River," as their opening chorus. Its last stanza ran as follows:

> "Oh the massa is proud of the old Broadhorn,
> For it brings him plenty of tin;
> Oh the crew, they are darkies, the cargo is corn,
> And the money comes tumbling in.
> There's plenty on board for de darkies to eat,
> And there's something to drink and to smoke;
> There's de banjo, de bones, and de tambourine,
> And de song, and de comical joke.
> Oh the river is up, and the channel is deep,
> And the wind blows steady and strong;
> Let the splash of your oars the measures keep,
> As we row de boat along.
>  Down the river, down the river;
>  Down the Ohio."

See *Christy's Bones and Banjo Melodies* (New York, 1864), pp. 11-12.

It was the interlocutor's business immediately to announce a ballad by one of the singers of the company, or to begin his chatter with the endman, the crude device which enabled the latter to get off his jokes and "pull his gags," to the great delight of the audience and to the apparent discomfort of the pompous interlocutor, whose intellectual standing always suffered in comparison with the nimble wits of the burnt cork stars on the ends. It was the duty of the interlocutor to bear the brunt of the jokes, and he received but little credit from the audience for the masterly manner in which he performed his task. On him depended the successful and smooth unfolding of the program of the show. The interlocutor had to introduce the entertainers, remember their lines, ask the proper questions at the proper time, laugh when necessary, answer all queries correctly, in short, carry the whole "first part" in his memory—helped only by the cues which he might have written out on the back of the fan which he carried in his hand. It has been suggested that this practice of having the interlocutor put down by the clever sallies of the endmen, amidst the boisterous laughter of the none too exacting audience, may have been borrowed from the circus, where the main function of the clowns is to bring the guffaws of the crowd down on the stately ringmaster.[2]

[2] Brander Matthews, *loc. cit.*, p. 756.

The interlocutor usually was a big man, and he always was attired in a large, full dress suit, or in some very conspicuous uniform. To make the contrast with the endmen more vivid, he neither blacked up nor wore the kinky wig of the Negro imitators. He played "straight." The first requirement for a successful interlocutor was a big, booming voice, for the success of the endmen's "gags" depended largely on the former's ability to make himself heard by the audience, and on his success in stringing out his questions and comments until the most stupid person among the listeners could not fail to grasp the point of the joke when it cracked at last from the big lips of the end man. The interlocutor was at once the announcer for the show and the "feeder to the comedians."

It should be pointed out at once that it did not require a high degree of intelligence to comprehend the jokes used in the average minstrel show. The point of many of them depended on that curious American trait which disdains even the appearance of too much intellectuality, and somehow, likes to see the triumph of the "low brow" over what it chooses to call the "high brow." "The crowd likes nothing better than to see a half-wit get the better of a pompous intellectual."[3] The interlocutor's func-

[3] Paskman and Spaeth, *op. cit.*, p. 26. Something of the same characteristic of Americans has been pointed out in quite another connection by James Truslow Adams, in "The Mucker Pose," *Harper's Magazine*, November, 1928, pp. 661-670.

tions became as stereotyped as the form of the show
he directed; even the formula for introducing the
balladists became fixed in a phrase like, "Mr. ———,
the popular tenor, will render ———'s famous ballad success, entitled ———." Occasionally, if the
interlocutor had a good voice, he might sing a ballad
himself. In that case, he was introduced to the audience by some member of the circle. He almost invariably participated in the singing of the chorus.

Originally, all endmen were addressed as "Mistah Tambo" and "Mistah Bones," names derived
from the instruments with which they added to the
hilarity and din of the show. Frank Brower, of the
original "Big Four," the Virginia Minstrels, seems
to have introduced the bones into minstrelsy. At
first, they were of bone, as the name implies; later
they were made of ebony or some other hard wood.
"Tambo," who performed on the tambourine, was
expected to go through wild and grotesque maneuvers for the benefit of the audience, while performing on his instrument.

As minstrelsy developed, the number of endmen
increased, until sometimes dozens of performers
graced the extremities of the half circle, and had to
be introduced to the audience in installments, the
greatest blackface stars naturally being reserved
for the last. Indeed, in many shows these did not
make their entry until well along toward the close

of the first part.   The endmen furnished the comedy of the show, and according to all accounts, from the beginning of minstrelsy to its decline as a form of professional theatricals, they were universally successful in keeping their audiences in an uproar, by their grimacing while the balladists were performing, by their own comic songs sung to the accompaniment of various clever or grotesque dance steps, which sometimes became indescribably eccentric gyrations, and by their rapid-fire jokes.   The apparent success of many of the latter defies all attempts at psychological explanation and analysis.

The endmen "made up" with big lips, a simple trick of rubbing the burnt cork first around their mouths, usually after a liberal admixture of saliva applied in the palm of the hand.   The burnt cork was then dusted off with a small brush.   Most performers exercised great care in fixing their mouths, for there was a rather widely accepted superstition among them that they would be unable to work properly in their acts unless this part of their make-up was perfect.   These big lips and the distended mouth helped to accentuate their shining white teeth.   A box of burnt cork was easily obtainable at twenty-five to fifty cents, wigs sold for twelve dollars a dozen, and special "scare" or "fright wigs," to make the hair stand on end at will, were available for six dollars.[4]

[4] Edward James, *op. cit.*

Endmen were expected to cultivate an eccentric vocabulary, full of bad grammar, faulty pronunciation and a kind of bombastic ignorance. On occasion too, the endmen might try to imitate Negroes who were particularly stupid and slow in grasping the meaning of words. The manifestation of characteristics supposedly peculiar to the Negro, like superstition and fear, also was counted on to produce the desired comedy effects. Clog dancing and soft shoe dancing, with many complicated steps and patterns, were introduced either as special features or during the chorus of the endmen's comic songs.

In the earliest days of minstrelsy, the emphasis was on the musical part of the show, and the singers in the semi-circle, generally in white face, entertained their listeners with ballads of every description. Some were sentimental portrayals of the joys and sorrows of slave life; others were saccharine love songs, full of maudlin sentimentality about almost any phenomenon in nature, or any human experience. Instrumental numbers were interspersed among the songs, and the violin in the early days of minstrelsy was in as great demand as the banjo. The comic songs and the farce comedy of the endmen was a somewhat later development; but once admitted into the first part, they quickly tended to crowd out the more purely musical features of the

program.   Burlesque opera, take-offs on stage and
public celebrities, and other specialties invaded even
this "first part" of the minstrel show.   In 1867,
Kelly and Leon began "Africanizing opera bouffe."
After anywhere from forty-five minutes to an hour
and a half of this mixture of music and comedy, the
first part came to a close, either with another song
and drill, or the "walk around" of all the performers, "the grand finale by the entire company," as the
interlocutor grandly announced.[5]

The scenic "sets" for these first parts were
fairly stereotyped during the early years of American minstrelsy.   Negro cabins by the cotton patch,
levees piled high with cotton bales, river boats, and
other scenes of the Southland, were popular always,
and most appropriate to the kind of performance the
original minstrel companies gave.   In the "mastodon," "gigantean," and "megatherian" companies of
later years, however, almost any elaborate setting
for the first part was satisfactory.   The emphasis
was on display and magnificence, both in costumes
and settings, regardless of their relationship to the
scenes where Negro minstrelsy originated.   First

[5] A popular closing chorus, used as late as 1911, but illustrative of
the kind of song used in earlier years also, was
  "Kiss your minstrel boy good-bye, babe, 'bye, babe, 'bye, babe,
  For the Pullman he must fly, babe, fly, babe, fly, babe,
  Be a good little girl, and a nice one too,
  Till your minstrel king comes back to you,
  Just kiss your minstrel boy good-bye."

part scenes which pleased audiences yearning for
gaudy colors and elaborate stage sets, included
scenes on board ships, lawn parties, military encamp-
ments, college campuses, Uncle Tom's Cabin, and
Broadway roof gardens and sky scrapers. The Field
Minstrels, in successive years beginning with 1901,
had "ten thousand dollar" first parts, with one hundred people on the stage, representing "The Paris
Exposition," "The Pan-American Exposition," and
"The Roof Garden—A Night in New York." Great
electrical effects with rain, wind and thunder, added
to the impressiveness of some of these costly displays.[6] For the forty-first and last season of the Al
G. Field Minstrels, "Up High" was the title given to
the scenic first part. It was prepared by the famous
scenic studio of M. Armbruster and Sons, who had
built stage settings for the Field show and other
minstrel companies for many years. In this last setting for the Field company the first part was en-
acted on top of a sky scraper, with a roof-garden
setting. In the exhilarating language of the press
agent, "In silhouette appear the topmost stories of
other tall buildings, inspiring monuments to the skill
of our craftsmen, their outlines softened by the sil-
very radiance of the full moon. . . . The varied
innovations introduced in this novel depiction of a
minstrel first part, stamp it as a black and white

[6] *The New York Clipper*, February 15, 1902.

revue of the most appealing type.   In this hour of
rapid entertainment, a melange of mirth and melody
par excellent [*sic*] is presented by a group of artists
unexcelled."

Another feature of minstrel performances was
the band and the street parade.   Whenever the minstrels came to town, their arrival was heralded by a
street parade, in which the "silver" or "gold cornet
band," gorgeously attired in colorful coats and trousers, big brass buttons and striking hats, led the procession through the streets of the town to the theatre, followed by the entire company, perhaps in long
Prince Albert coats or swallow-tails, with fancy
vests or colored lapels, and high silk "plug" hats.
The parade usually proceeded in two's or four's, depending on the size of the company.   Every effort
was made to draw it out to the greatest possible
length.   Here was the drum major in attractive regi-
mentals whirling his baton as only modern leaders
of college bands can do, leading the minstrel boys,
two or four abreast, silk hatted, caned and bouton-
niered, swinging down the street with almost a tip-
toe step.   In front of the theatre the band gave a
short concert before each performance, and sometimes fireworks were shot off for the edification of
the crowd and the street urchins of the town.

What a day it was when the minstrels came to

town! First the excitement of the gaudy, grotesque lithographs and posters put up in every strategic place by the skillful advance agent. And how the town resounded to the blare of the minstrel band, as it swung down the street to the tune of old favorites, like "Dixie," "Carve Dat Possum," "The Natchez and the Robert E. Lee," or "A Hot Time in the Old Town," while the crowd assembled before the "Opera House" to greet their favorites of "the burnt cork opry" circle.

The minstrel parade is another example of the close relationship between the circus and minstrel shows. It was borrowed directly from the circus parade, and became an established part of every minstrel outfit in America. Mexican drum majors, pickanniny drum corps, and silken banners, great capes and gold-headed canes frequently were special features of these parades.[7] In 1896, D. W. McCabe's Young Operatic Minstrels staged "a Turkish bath parade," with four lady buglers on horseback, twelve dancing musketeers, six drum majors, two drummers, an eighteen piece band, and various animals.[8] While the origin of this feature of minstrelsy is sometimes accredited to Ordway's Minstrels and the Christy Company, in about the year

[7] *The New York Clipper,* September 5, 1896.
[8] *Ibid.*

1850,[9] Al G. Field claimed to have been the first manager to uniform the minstrels in the parade in long, light-colored, newmarket overcoats with black velvet collars, in contrast with the red, broadcloth, trimmed uniforms worn by the band.[10]   In a number of seasons, Field had Shetland ponies and Arabian horses in his minstrel parades.[11]

By 1850, the form of the American minstrel show had become immutably fixed, as far as the minstrel semi-circle first part, and a second part variety bill, called the olio, were concerned.   The last act in this olio, or second part, in the early days represented a genuine, hilarious darky "hoe-down" in which every member of the company did a dance at the center of the stage, while the others sang and vigorously clapped their hands to emphasize the rhythm.   For some years there also was a third part, consisting of farce, comic opera, or burlesque, but this was gradually merged with the other acts of the olio.

[9] See Paskman and Spaeth, *op. cit.,* p. 19.
[10] Field, *Watch Yourself Go By,* p. 500.
[11] For working models of minstrel shows, see Paskman and Spaeth, *op. cit.,* pp. 97-151; Frank Dumont, *The Whitmark Amateur Minstrel Guide and Burnt Cork Encyclopedia* (New York, 1899) ; *Bobby Newcomb's Guide to the Minstrel Stage,* advertised for one dollar in *The New York Clipper,* March 11, 1871; Herbert Preston Powell, *The World's Best Book of Minstrelsy* (Philadelphia, 1926) ; Cecil H. Bullivant, *Home Fun* (New York, 1910) ; and Walter B. Hare, *The Minstrel Encyclopedia* (Boston, 1921).   These books contain many minstrel sketches, and as their titles imply, are intended to instruct amateurs who wish to put on minstrel shows.

As minstrelsy prospered in the last half of the
nineteenth century, all kinds of new features were
introduced, especially into the olio, until it became a
medley of acts little different from the ordinary
burlesques or variety show bill, and without any
necessary relationship to Negro plantation life. Perhaps in view of the present-day interest in Negro
folklore and folkmusic, minstrelsy might have lived
longer had it confined itself more rigidly to a presentation of Negro types and Negro scenes, and re-
jected all the extraneous matter which was invading
its programs and robbing it of its earlier unique
features.  On the other hand, of course, it may be
maintained that minstrel managers accepted these
innovations only because they found it necessary to
compete with other forms of entertainment for
which the public seemed to manifest a greater
interest.

This transformation of the olio in American
minstrel productions became apparent very early in
the history of minstrelsy, and proceeded rapidly during more recent decades.  In New Orleans, as early
as 1845, a company of minstrels presented, after a
traditional first part, an olio containing two trained
dogs, a comic song by Sam S. Sanford, classic
groupings, and a burlesque opera called "The Virginia Girl, or a Nigger's Love."  There followed

"Monsieur Cassimir, the Great French Drummer," who played on a drum "his original imitation of the field of battle at Rio Grande—firing of musketry, and the cannonading of General Taylor's army, on the night of the 9th of May," depicting the advance, retreat and ultimate slaughter of the Mexicans in that bloody encounter, a performance which must have stirred the audience to applause because the war was then still in progress. After this series of imitations, the company staged "A grand Trial of Skill," in which two banjo players contended "for the championship in their unrivalled banjo solos," and concluded with "The Ethiopian Serenader's Concert" and a grand match dance between Sanford and Swayne Buckley, two of minstrelsy's most famous eccentric dancers. All this mélange was presented for an admission of from twenty-five to fifty cents per person.[12]

A play bill of Ordway's Aeolians for 1851, when that organization played for one hundred and fifty nights in Boston, shows that the performance was divided into four parts. In the first part, the troupe appeared dressed as ordinary citizens, and in white face. In Part II, they were "made up" as Northern darkies. In both the first and second parts of the program, the company presented songs and comedy conforming rather closely to the pattern of the tradi-

[12] *The New York Clipper*, September 29, 1877.

tional "first part." Part III consisted of what may be called a concert, in which popular gems from operas like *The Bohemian Girl, Lucia di Lammermoor,* and *La Sonnambula* were presented. In only the last part did the company appear as Southern darkies, with bone and accordeon solos, banjo duets, dances like "Lucinda Snow," and other Negro imitations.[13] The program of the Ethiopian Serenaders for their performance of November 6, 1861, in Columbus, Ohio, was divided into three parts. The first was devoted mainly to music, and the performers appeared in ordinary citizen's dress. Part II included various musical numbers, a tyrolean quartette with burlesque imitations, the song and dance, "Lucy Long" in bloomer costumes, "the laughable Black Shakers," banjo numbers, and plantation jigs. The third section consisted of a Dutch drill, lectures on phrenology and mesmerism, burlesques of Shakespearean scenes, and a finale entitled "Well's Original Burlesque Lecture on Animal Magnetism."[14]

The program of Bryant's Minstrels, advertised as "The Excelsior Troupe of the World," for the performance of September 12, 1859, is of special interest because it was on this occasion that "Dixie" was introduced to an American audience. The program consisted of a number of ballads and comic

[13] *The New York Clipper,* May 28, 1871.
[14] See *Ohio State Journal,* February 25, November 6, and 11, 1851.

songs for the first part, a bill of varieties, which included a violin solo, a burlesque African polka and a "Flutina Fantasia" by Neil Bryant, for the second part, and for the closing number, a burlesque Italian opera, the cast consisting of Mlle. Pickie Hominy, Prima Donna, Count no Count McCaffery, Primo Tenor, Sig. Houlahau Stuffhisowni, Primo Basso, Sig. Sardinero, and other names equally ludicrous.[15]

In 1871, Skiff and Gaylord's Minstrels, playing at Mozart Hall in Cincinnati for three nights, appeared in white face for the first two performances and in blackface only for their last appearance. "After each performance, a panorama of the Franco-Prussian War (then still technically in progress) was exhibited."[16] Bryant's Minstrels, playing in New York in 1877, presented an olio of song and dance numbers, a falsetto ballad singer, a musical sketch called "Crochets and Quavers," with banjo variations, sketches of "The Happy Family," and "The Wrong Man," and closed with Dan Emmett's famous walk-around, "Dixie's Land," by the entire company. A company at the Bowery Theatre early in the same decade featured plantation scenes and Negro character acts, and closed with a "terrific steamboat explosion."[17]

[15] A photostat of this program may be found in Rice, *Monarchs of Minstrelsy*, p. 185.
[16] *The New York Clipper*, March 11, 1871.
[17] *Ibid.*, June 10, 1871.

In 1884, Haverly's Mastodon Minstrels, with
sixty visible performers, nearly a score of endmen
with tambourines and bones, and a half dozen special
stars who appeared on the ends in relays, played at
the Drury Lane Theatre in London. The promoter,
Colonel Haverly, the P. T. Barnum of the minstrel
business, did not hesitate to introduce Irish comedy
songs in the olio, as well as acrobats and clog dancers
who appeared in shining armor in what was called
the "Silver Combat Clog Dance." Neither in the
ballads nor in the afterpiece was there much of that
Negro cunning and simplicity which once marked
the performances of the earliest Negro minstrels.[18]

Al G. Field opened his first minstrel show in
Marion, Ohio, on October 6, 1886, with an afterpiece called "The Lime Kiln Club," a pretentious
stage setting representing the interior of a lodge
room, with antiquated furniture, a large sheet iron
stove, and other equipment. Field spent a great deal
of money and energy on stage equipment, and began
the practice of carrying complete scenic sets and
other stage paraphernalia with him in a special railroad car, instead of relying on the sets available in
local theatres. To the end of his career, his elaborate sets, made by the firm of M. Armbruster and
Sons of Columbus, Ohio, were the envy of his many
competitors.[19]

[18] *The Saturday Review*, LVII, 740.
[19] Field, *Watch Yourself Go By*, 501 ff.

For the season of 1897, Field used a one hour burlesque, entitled "Utopia," in which eight Shetland ponies and two Arabian horses appeared on the stage.[20]    There were seventy members in his minstrel troupe in that year.    The year before, Field had celebrated his tenth anniversary as owner of a minstrel show, and had announced with pardonable pride that he had never failed to meet a financial obligation, a statement that could not have been truthfully made by some of his competitors.    In honor of this special occasion, new brocaded satin suits of special excellence were provided for the first part, and Field himself, with Donnelly, one of his star comedians, appeared in a burlesque of "Trilby," Field representing Svengali and Donnelly the harassed heroine of the Latin quarter.[21]    Field's costuming, always very gorgeous, was designed and supervised for many years by his niece, Pearl Field, who traveled with the show.

For 1897-98, Field planned a show which should present in panorama the whole history of the colored race.    It contained such scenes as a cotton field with a cotton gin in operation, a Louisiana sugar plantation, the levee at New Orleans, and a panorama of the Mississippi, showing the famous race between the *Natchez* and the *Robert E. Lee.*    Other sets rep-

[20] *The New York Clipper,* March 7, 1896.
[21] *Ibid.,* January 18, 1896.

resented the interior of the South Carolina State House at the time of the Hayes-Tilden election dispute in 1876, a gambling scene, a camp meeting, Jacksonville, Florida, on the night of the Corbett-Mitchell prize fight, and a ball room scene in Negro high life in Washington, D. C. Oliver Scott and Al G. Field were the promoters and proprietors of this gigantic production, known as "Darkest America." The show, it was announced, would consist entirely of colored performers, and would play only one week stands. The special scenery for this elaborate and costly display was carried in two seventy-foot railroad cars. In 1896, a similar, but somewhat less pretentious offering had played for twenty-eight weeks in fourteen different states, traveling over twelve thousand miles.[22]

When Primrose and West's Minstrels, another of minstrelsy's premier organizations, opened at Long Island in the fall of 1896, their olio contained a musical act called "Fun in a Post Office," a cornet soloist, various medleys and parodies, and a company of colored pickaninnies.[23] Barlow Brothers' Minstrels, who opened in Petersburg, Virginia, in the same year, carried a juggler and a contortionist as special features of the olio. In the first part, the performers sang a medley of national airs, "America

[22] *The New York Clipper,* January 18, 1896.
[23] *Ibid.,* September 5, 1896.

All Through," with all the singers attired in satin suits of stars and stripes.[24]   An annual feature at the Eleventh Street Opera House, where Dumont's Minstrels held forth as a permanent company, was the distribution of Christmas toys and candies from a large Christmas tree to the children at a special Christmas matinee.[25]   The same troupe presented special burlesques, "Who Owns the Streets, or Digging up Philadelphia," and "The Cold Storage Trolley Cars, or a Freeze to Death Trip," at a time when the city was suffering from a prolonged controversy with its traction company.[26]

Lew Dockstader's company, during one season, ended the first part of its program with a farce entitled, "Shakespeare or Bacon—Which," with a cast composed of "Ignatius Donnelly, Mr. Sturdevant, Dumpy, Hamlet, Romeo, Juliet, Mr. Paris, Macbeth, and Macduff."[27]   Another novelty in 1911, representing an interesting attempt to combine minstrelsy with the moving picture, much in the fashion of the recent "talkies," was the Spook Minstrels, in which five men in colonial costumes and powdered wigs sang ballads while moving pictures of a regulation first part were thrown on a screen, the real singers talking and singing to the accompaniment of the

[24] *The New York Clipper,* September 5, 1896.
[25] *Ibid.,* December 28, 1901.
[26] *Ibid.,* November 16, 1901.
[27] *Ibid.,* April 8, 1911.

moving figures. At the end of the first part, the
screen was raised and the five singers were revealed
to the audience.[28]

The olio thus became a vaudeville show, with
monologues, song and dance numbers, musical and
instrumental acts, and short burlesques, and all unity
was sacrificed in this series of variety acts. Club
and hoop manipulators, acrobats, animal acts, a drill
and dance entitled "The Colored Knights of Labor,"
big watermelon parties, monologists billed as "The
Black Demosthenes" and holding forth on timely
topics like "Carrie Nation, the Masher" (in 1901),
yodellers, burnt-cork artists doing skits like "The
Old Clothes Man" in Hebrew dialect and others in
Irish brogue, excellent or mediocre musical acts,
usually with one or more performers showing their
dexterity on a number of instruments, the champion
heavyweight pugilist, John L. Sullivan, appearing in
classical poses to represent ancient statuary (1885-6),
expert whistlers and imitators of birds and animals
of every kind, contortionists, pantomimes and
shadow pictures, songs illustrated with stereopticon
slides, perhaps to the accompaniment of a banjo,—
these and scores of other features comprised the
olios of minstrel shows of modern times. In 1927,

[28] *Ibid.*, May 6, 1911. Occasionally, minstrel troupes carried large
canvas tents and a staff of workingmen and bill posters with them,
and presented their show in certain localities after the fashion of the
traveling circus. (*Ibid.*, March 8, 1902.)

the afterpiece of one of the last Field Minstrel productions was the Negro absurdity, "The Spook's Rendezvous," based on the superstitions of the southern Negro, the scene of the action being a swamp in Florida which was filled with mysterious voices and "hants."[29]

Occasionally, a minstrel travesty, like Field's satire on the craze for baseball, "Darktowns vs. Slapjacks," had real value, and was carefully worked out to ridicule or draw attention to certain passing fads, while the take-offs on theatrical stars and on the more serious plays and operas often displayed rare powers of mimicry. "Daddy" Rice was famous for his presentation of "Sarah Heartburn," an imitation of the stage technique and mannerisms of Sarah Bernhard, and on one occasion, he delighted the noted tragedienne herself with his mimicry. Lew Dockstader, one of the last of the minstrel stars, was popular for his burlesque of *Camille*. Lew Ratter and Johnny De Angeles, who performed for years on the Pacific coast, specialized in burlesques of Shakespeare and comic opera travesties. *Romeo and Juliet* became "Roman Nose and Suet"; *Othello*, "Old Fellow, or the Boor of Vengeance"; *Macbeth*, "Bad Breath, the Crane of Chowder"; and *Camille*, "Clameel, or the Feet of a Go-Getter."[30]

[29] For other examples, see *The New York Clipper*, September 5, 1896; March 11, 1911; December 14, 1901; May 20, 1911; February 8, 1902; March 8, 1902; and Rice, *op. cit.*, pp. 92, 339, 290, 182, 118.
[30] E. T. Sawyer, "Old Time Minstrels in San Francisco," p. 5.

Various dancing stunts were performed as part of the olio, such as dancing on a peck measure or on a small square of glass, one inch thick, often in competition with other famous terpsichorean artists, and at these tournaments of skill, according to a theatre magnate of the late nineteenth century, "there was as much excitement as might be caused today by a great automobile contest."[31] More recently, minstrel shows contained "pleasing dancing diversions," affording "opportunity for an expression of graceful glides and synchronous stepping, in keeping with the moonlit plantation background."[32] Finally, female minstrels also enjoyed considerable vogue. Numerous troupes toured the country, and probably did little to keep minstrelsy from sinking to the level of cheap burlesque "girl" shows.[33] As late as the fall of 1929, Jack Curtis and Marvin Welt were producing a thirty-five girl minstrel show, to be known as the Honey Girl Minstrels, and booked for the RKO vaudeville houses. One of the special features of this new organization was to be an old-time street parade, at 11:45 in the morning, and a band concert in front of the theatre.

[31] Leavitt, *op. cit.*, pp. 33-34.

[32] From a Field Minstrels press notice of 1927.

[33] Among the better known companies of female minstrels were Thomas P. Kelley's Big Lady Minstrels, Mme. Rentz's, Ford and Green's, Alice Gilmore's, and Minnie Wells' Female Minstrels. See *The New York Clipper,* June 10, 1871, March 11, 1871, January 18, 1902.

It is quite impossible to give an adequate conception of the kind of jokes that characterized the comedy of the minstrel performers, whether in the earliest days of their profession or during more recent times when their art was declining rapidly. Joke books are available for various periods, and they may be consulted by any one particularly interested in this kind of humor. But it must be pointed out at once that some of the best bits of buffoonery never were reduced to the printed page.

Many of these attempts at humor by the minstrel boys were as inane as those "cracked" by comedians in the present-day extravaganza, girl show, comic opera, or vaudeville performance. They depended for their success to a very large degree on the personality of the performer and on the particular method of delivery, a matter which cannot be described, even if more information about the technique of individual endmen were available. Many of the old minstrel stars have left little but their names and a few fleeting newspaper records of their great popularity. Moreover, a minstrel with a speech of a dozen lines probably never made it twice in exactly the same way,—a good minstrel was always improvising, and adding little comic bits on the spur of the moment while the show was in full progress, quite as much for the amusement of his fellow-members in the company, as for the audience.

The endman's chatter with the interlocutor usually varied to a greater or less degree, from night to night, and many stories and jokes about the local community were introduced with real skill. Some companies actually sent advance agents ahead to pick up bits of local news to be used in their show for the peculiar delight of their special audiences. But after all due allowance has been made for the fact that these jokes and minstrel dialogues undoubtedly gained a good deal from the gestures, costumes, and vocal tricks of the performers, many of them, when reduced to cold type, must strike the reader of today as rather futile or far-fetched attempts at comedy.[34]

Family relationships, with all their complexities and irritations, and with special reference to fathers- and mothers-in-law, and others of the wife's relatives, and allusions to the difficulties of the married state, furnished much of the comedian's inspiration, in the heyday of minstrelsy, as they do today in the burlesque and musical comedies. Woman's rights and the equality of the sexes was another fertile field to be exploited in the nineteenth century, when this great question still aroused considerable debate. It was as full of possibilities for the comedian in that period as prohibition is to the present generation. George Christy, for example, introduced a dialogue between Sam and Julius about love and doughnuts,

[34] See for example, an extract in Minnigerode, *op. cit.,* pp. 235-236.

a rather inane bit which seems to have been especially popular with theatre-goers two generations ago.  It pictured the wife of one of the endmen, returning to her home after hours spent at a woman's rights convention (still quite a novelty in the period of the Civil War when this skit was used).  When her husband pleaded for his favorite pastry, the irate spouse broke out, "Inferior sex!  If you want doughnuts, cook 'em yourself."  The husband concluded the debate with the shout, "Bloomerizical female, if de price ob doughnuts is to be de liberty of my sex, the bargain's off, and so am I!"  From contemporaneous accounts one must conclude that this retort drove the audiences of the 1860's into gales of laughter.[35]

Another popular hit in these earlier years consisted of the endman reproducing a scene between a rather belligerent wife and her boastful but timid husband.  The former arrived just in time to overhear her husband's remarks about who is "boss" in the home.  After a long exchange of anything but pleasantries, the debate usually ended by the amazon dragging "her nigger" off the stage by the ear, amid the jeers and applause of the not too exacting audience.[36]

Conundrums and puns have always been the

[35] *George Christy's Essence of Old Kentucky* (New York, 1864), pp. 69-70.
[36] Rice, *op. cit.*, p. 2.

stock in trade of minstrel comedians. Here, in particular, local characters and situations could be cleverly introduced. "Why is Henry Ward Beecher like Brigham Young," queried the interlocutor during the years when the great preacher and the apostle of Mormonism were equally well known to American audiences. "Because he has married a great many women and keeps marrying more," snapped back the endman.[37]

Sixty years before a distinguished university president, in his plea for higher salaries for professors, made striking use of the old pun, the minstrels had pointed out that "the difference between a schoolmaster and an engineer is that one trains the mind and the other minds the train."[38]   Baseball contributed a whole flock of puns and jokes to minstrelsy when it became the American national sport. The pun about the new pitcher, named "Dice," because he's hard to "rattle," is but one example of an almost endless collection. Endmen explained how they got rich collecting hush money from the town's most respected family—by selling soothing syrup; and in the days of the Civil War, when war taxes were imposed upon almost all articles of general consumption, the comedian explained that he had "to stamp his feet" when he put on his shoes each morning.

[37] *Christy's Bones and Banjo Melodist*, p. 55.
[38] *George Christy's Essence of Old Kentucky*, p. 59.

To satirize Horace Greeley's intense and almost fanatical interest in the abolitionist movement, a dialogue between two Negroes concerning some wonderful eggs was presented in one of the minstrel shows at the beginning of the Civil War. One of the comedians, after a long discussion, finally opened a box supposed to contain the remarkable "hen fruit." Of course, he was greatly shocked when he found that the box contained not eggs, but a live Negro. The frightened darky started running off the stage, shouting for Greeley. At this point the interlocutor intervened with the query of "what did he want with Horace Greeley?" so that the endman could reply, "He said dat he want to see Horace Greeley, for he had a box of eggs to sell him—dat ebery egg would hatch a nigger!"[39] Imitating the supposed obtuseness and stupidity of the Negro race, another endman explained to the attentive interlocutor how he "got the best" of a railroad company, by buying a return ticket without intending to use it; or how, in order to be near his brother who was serving in the sixth regiment in the United States Army, he had asked to be put into the seventh. If the audience proved particularly responsive to this kind of entertainment, the dialogue between the interlocutor and the comedian might close with a discussion of the question why "niggers" make the

[39] *George Christy's Essence of Old Kentucky*, p. 59.

best soldiers. The answer was that they were "fast colors and never run."[40]

Another favorite device of the endmen was to entertain their audiences with the recital of a poem, or with a speech, usually on a topic that was utterly nonsensical, and adorned with puns galore. One example of this particular type of recitation, in which punning predominated, will suffice.

> I've seen the *rope-walk* down the lane,
>     The *sheep-run* in the vale;
> I've seen the *dog-watch* on the ship,
>     The *cow-slip* in the dale;
> I've seen the *sea-foam* at the mouth,
>     The *horse-fly* in the air;
> I know the *bul-warks* on the deck,
>     And the *fire-works* many a scare;
> I've seen *a-bun-dance* on the plate,
>     A *lamp-light* on the floor;
> I've seen the *cat-fish* in the sea,
>     And a *hat-stand* by the door;
> I've seen the *mill-race* on the glen,
>     The *heart-burn* in the breast;
> I've seen a *door-step* on the street,
>     And a *watch-spring* in my vest.[41]

The old effusion about

> The boy stood on the burning deck,
>     Whence all but him had fled, etc.,

lent itself to almost an infinite number of variations. Frequently the interlocutor would recite this popular

[40] See Dumont, *Minstrel Guide*, pp. 55-60.
[41] *Ibid.*, p. 56.

favorite correctly, in order to give the endman the opportunity to improve on his rendition, by such new versions as the following,

> The boy stood in the farmer's field,
> And ate with great dispatch,
> Of all the sturdy vine did yield
> Within that melon patch.
> Yes, beautiful and bright he stood,
> With colic yet unknown;
> Yet soon the hills and dusky wood,
> Did echo back his groan.[42]

And so on, for endless stanzas.

Of all living mortals, the barber probably furnished as much inspiration for the minstrel comedian as any other human being. Witness the following sample of punning skill, delivered in rapid-fire tempo, utterly "senseless, but apparently popular" with the audiences of the days of our fathers and grandfathers. The endman chattered,

In about ten minutes in *comb* the barber. He entered all of a *lather,* and said he'd just give his boss a *strapping,* and got fired out. He said he'd just got *shaved* of all his money, and would like to make a stake somewhere, and wanted to know if I knew where he could *rais'er.* It looked to me as though he was making a *cut* to borrow a dollar, and as I didn't like the looks of his *mug,* I told him he better *oil* up and git.[43]

On the same high level are the endless puns of later days about the girl who looked up in the eyes of her

[42] Dumont, *Minstrel Guide,* p. 48.
[43] Ed. James, *The Amateur Negro Minstrel Guide,* pp. 20-22.

young man and called him her "shining light," until
the father came and "put him out," and the gallant
youth outwitted them all by going away "smoking."

It is apparent from the above illustrations that
many of the most popular jokes in minstrel performances had nothing whatsoever to do with Negro life,
nor were they in any way peculiar to minstrelsy.
Although there were many conundrums, puns, and
humorous situations depending for their comic success on the Negro's love for big words, his clumsy
mispronunciations, and his obtuseness, the jokesters
of minstrelsy, like the comedians of the present day,
claimed the whole world for their province. Endmen's "gags" frequently dealt with Negro life, but
the blackface comedian by no means was limited to
that field. Everything from mothers-in-law to prohibition, from Nero to Calvin Coolidge, from Adam
and Eve to Einstein, from the marriage relation to
relativity, was utilized in the endless search for
"new" comic material.

It would be interesting to learn how many original themes there really are in the long history of
jokes and "funny stories," or just who it was who
first "pulled" one of the most characteristic minstrel
"gags" of all time, the familiar query, "Who was
that lady I saw you with last night?" The endman
always explained, as jokesters may have explained
for centuries before him, that she really wasn't a

lady, but only his wife. In the long history of minstrel shows the comedians, in their ceaseless hunt for new material, must have worn every one of the possible variations of the old themes completely threadbare.[44]

Scores of "joke books" were printed year after year during the decades when minstrelsy flourished, and these collections were available to the public at the modest price of ten to twenty-five cents a copy.[45] Let the reader pick up any of the minstrel joke-books, like Jack Haverly's *Negro Minstrels,* published in Chicago in 1902, or W. B. Dick's *Ethiopian Scenes,* of 1879, and he will find not only complete directions for staging a minstrel performance, but jokes, gags, stump speeches, variety sketches, popular songs, and conundrums which will lead him irresistibly to the conclusion that there can be little new or original among the professional jokesters, and that there are few of the stage conundrums, or even farce and comedy situations of today which cannot be connected with minstrels whose names have long been forgotten.  Such collections of American wit and humor were sold under various titles; such as, *Black Wit and Darkey Conversations, Charley Fox's Ethiopian Comicalities,* and *Laughing Gas or Wit, Wisdom and Wind.*

[44] For other examples, see *The New York Clipper,* May 28, 1871; Paskman and Spaeth, *op. cit.,* pp. 80-86; and Charles Townsend, *Negro Minstrels; with endmen's jokes, etc.* (Chicago, 1891).

[45] See for example, an advertisement in *George Christy's Essence of Old Kentucky.*

The monologue, or "stump speech" as it was known originally, generally followed the first part, as the first act in the olio. This order in the program became fixed by a tradition which was seldom violated. This act usually fell to the company's premier blackface comedian, and was a somewhat more advanced state of fun-making than the dialogues of endmen and interlocutors in the first part. From the days of Dan Emmett to modern stars, like Lew Dockstader and Bert Swor, the monologue was the high spot in the evening's entertainment. Clever lines and comic material of the more traditional sort were skillfully interwoven with pungent comments on local celebrities and public affairs, local, national, and international. Politics, of course, was a specially fruitful field, and much of the success of the monologue depended on impromptu sallies in which real blackface stars excelled.

A Negro sermon delivered as a stump speech by Dan Emmett fortunately has been preserved, and a selection from this monologue may be quoted as an example of "stump speaking" in the early days of minstrelsy, by one of the pioneers of the blackface art.

"Bredren," Emmett began,

De text am foun' in de inside ob Job whar Paul draw'd him a pistol on 'Feesians, lebenteenth chapter, an' no 'ticklar verse: "Bressed am dem dat 'spects nuttin', kaze dey aint gwine to git nuttin'."

After many digressions, Emmett finally "got to lassly," and closed with,

I sees a great many heah dis ebenin' dat cares no moa what 'comes of darr souls dan I does myseff. Suppose, frinstance, dat yoa eat yoa full ob possam fat an' hominy; yoa go to bed, an' in de mornin' yoa wake up an' find youseff dead! Whar yoa speck yoa gwine to? Yoa keep gwine down, down, down, till de bottam falls out! What 'comes ob ye den? You see de debble comein' down de hill on a rasslejack, wid a ear like a backer leaf an' a tail like a cornstalk; out of de mouff comes pitchforks an' lightnin', an' him tail smoke like a tar kill! Whar is you now? No time for 'pentin'; de debble kotch ye, shoa! but bress de lam', he habn't kotch dis child yet! What's gwine to 'come ob ye on de great gittin'-up-day? Maby yoa tink you hold on to my coat-tail; but I'm gwine to fool yoa bad on dat 'casion, kaze I'm gwine to wear my coon-skin jacket! Yoa crawl, up de hill on yoa han's an' 'nees, yoa fall down again, wallup! . . . den yoa's call'd a backslider. Dar's de brimstone, de grindstone, de millstone, de blue stone, an eb'ry udder kind o' stone de debble's got to tie 'roun' yoa neck, to sink ye in de nebberlastin' gulf ob bottomless ruin. Yoa call for a cup of cold water an' de debble say "No!" . . . Den yoa weep an 'wail an' smash out yoa teef out. Den wake up, sinners, an' let de daybroke in on ye!

My fren's, I neider preach for de lob ob de lam', de good ob yoa souls, nor de fear ob de debble; but, if you got any ole shoe, ole coat, ole hat, jiss pass 'em 'roun' dis way, an' I'll light upon 'em like a raccoon upon a green cornstalk. It's no use passin' 'roun de plate for "Bressed am dem dat 'specks nuttin' kaze dey ain't a gwine to git nuttin'."[46]

The number of subjects on which stump speeches or monologues could be worked out were great in-

[46] Charles Burleigh Galbreath, *Daniel Decatur Emmett*, pp. 44-45.

deed, but topics like "Are Women more Beautiful than Men," "Goats," "On Love," "Woman's Tongue," "Adam and Eve," and many effusions on matrimony, politics, and public affairs always were popular. A favorite was "A Sermon on Keards, Hosses, Fiddlers and Foolin' with the Gals." A parody stump speech on "Mark Anthony's Oration," ended, "When the poor hath cried, Caesar hath wept, because it didn't cost anything, and it made him solid with the gang. . . . You all know this ulster; I remember the first time Caesar put it on."[47] Another, "On Patriotism," was full of allusions to pressing public issues. "All we want am offis," and "we got in for de biggest of liberty—liberty to do nothin' as much as we like, an' get well paid for it." "Our lub of country is 'bove eberything 'cept trade dollars. . . . We belieb' in universal suff'rin, dat all men am free an' equal, 'cept Chinese washermen 'cause dey hab no vote. We lub de Irisher, Scotty, Englisher, Dutchy Greesers, Frenchy an' half Spanish, when dey wote as we say dey shall. We guv up hangin' de nigger 'cause ob his good 'Merican vote!" "Carl Shoots (Schurz) what am his sentiments?" the black Demosthenes continued, with a sally about that statesman's notorious independence in party politics. "Any side is de best which got de gibin' out ob de pickings," he answered. "Who cares for de

<hr>

[47] Dumont, *Minstrel Guide*, pp. 85-86, and James, *op. cit.*, p. 181.

wooden-legged soldier man?" shot out the next question, with an obvious reference to pensions for Civil War veterans. "Hand-organ good enough for him —man who shot his leg off must be put on de pay-roll ob de Norf till de Souf gets a better pay-roll! Dat am de only justice made nowadays—justice winkin' one eye, wid one side de scales 'way up, an' de oder 'way down. . . ."[48]

Frequently, the monologist broke into verse. Witness "Uncle Pete's Sermon," which began:

Belubbed fellow-trabblers, in holding for' today,
I doesn't quote no special verse for what I has to say;
De sarmon will be very short, and dis here am de tex;
Dat half-way doin's ain't no 'count, for dis world, or de nex'.
Dis world dat we's a libbin in is like a cotton row,
Whar ebbry cullud gemman has got his line to hoe;
An' ebbry time a lazy nigger stops to take a nap,
De grass keeps on a-growin', to smudder up his crap. . . .

And Uncle Pete concluded his poetic exhortation:

I t'anks you for de 'tention you hab gib dis arternoon,
Sister Williams will 'blige us by de raisin' ob a tune;
I see dat Brudder Johnson's 'bout to pass 'round de hat,
And don't let's hab no half-way doin's when it comes to dat.[49]

Minstrel shows, as has been pointed out earlier, always made much of their concert features. In the language of a modern press agent, "singing is the sheet anchor of minstrelsy," and "the plaintive melo-

---

[48] James, *op. cit.,* p. 16.
[49] *Dick's Ethiopian Scenes* (New York, 1879), p. 108.

dies of the Southland, mingled with the peppy tunes of today, the levee dances of slavery days and the daring dances of today go to make a modernized minstrel mélange entertaining to all." "Without singing spirited, harmonious vocal effects, the atmosphere of minstrelsy would be lost." To most recent times, minstrel programs contained the newest popular "hits," with a judicious admixture of "the heart songs to inspire memories of the old-time show."

Minstrel songs appeared during the heyday of the minstrel business almost as fast as the music publishing houses could turn them out for the eager public. The earliest of them survive in collections like *The Nigga Singer's Own Book, Christy's and White's Ethiopian Melodies,* various *Ethiopian Glee Books,* and *Marsh's Selection, or, Singing for the Million, Containing the Choicest and Best Collection of Admired Patriotic, Comic, Irish, Negro, Temperance, and Sentimental Songs Ever Embodied in One Work* (New York, 1854). Some of the earliest compositions and minstrel melodies were reminiscent of the southern camp meetings, or had their origin in the melodies sung by wagoners, cattle-drivers, and other itinerants of the middle nineteenth century. To the extent that this was true, they had some value, aside from their musical merits, as part

of the folkmusic of the nation.[50]   Some of these
songs were sheer nonsense, others the last word in
cheap, tawdry sentimentality.

Some of the earliest minstrel songs which delighted the audiences of two or three generations ago
have both a sentimental and historical value, and
should be given a significant place in any account of
the musical development of the United States.   This
is especially true of the compositions of Stephen C.
Foster, B. R. Hanby, A. T. Bryant, James E. Stew-
art, Will S. Hays, L. V. H. Crosby, James A. Bland,
Charles A. White, Luke Schoolcraft, Henry C.
Work, and S. S. Steele.   Their musical compositions,
distinctively American, probably could have been
written in no other country, for they were based
upon the minstrel's conception of the life of slavery
days, and sought to express its spirit and its sentiment, the amusements, the simple interests, the deep-
rooted attachment of the Negro race to a peculiar
locality.   But the music of these composers has little
if any resemblance to the so-called Negro music so
much in vogue today, unless one encounters a clear
case of borrowing from the minstrel stage.   Many
of the early minstrel songs retained a deep under-
tone of sentiment and much of the Negro racial

[50] See for example, the excellent collection of Carl Sandburg, *The
American Song Bag* (New York, 1927), especially pp. 47-51, where
some of the old-time minstrel songs are reprinted.   The whole collection is really a source book in American social history.

strain, and in this sense differed greatly from the
parlor ballads of the same period.

Most of these minstrel songs were written by
white men; some of the composers were minstrel
performers; others had little contact with actual
plantation life except through their vivid and sentimental imaginations. They created "a *genre* which
cannot be described as a folk-song, although it has
the folk-song feeling, nor as art-song, nor yet merely
as popular ballad." Their melody was simple, and
their harmonies and rhythm very elementary. Perhaps originally this type of composition was an attempt at an artistic rendition of music heard among
the slaves, but it was not long until the real Negro
song was so idealized and blended with the flavor of
the parlor ballad that the popular Negro minstrel
song of the strongly sentimental kind was produced.
Even Stephen Foster's songs, generally regarded as
saturated with the feeling of the Negro, were the
creations of a composer who had never lived in the
South except for a visit of a few days in Kentucky,
until after most of his songs had appeared. In the
"walk-around," in the course of which the whole
minstrel company stood in a semi-circle and, one at
a time, advanced to the center of the stage to do his
song and dance after having "walked around" the
inside of the circle several times, a peculiar kind of

music was utilized, and this style affected compositions for the minstrel stage for many years.[51]

Recent investigations, notably by Professor Newman I. White, of Duke University, into the origins of Negro secular folksongs have revealed "the white man in the woodpile." Since a surprisingly large element in these songs has its origin outside the Negro race, it may be worth while to refer again to the great number of minstrel and dance songs by which white composers and actors, particularly around the middle of the last century, seem to have influenced the Negro's secular music. The principal minstrel performers were white men, and many of them wrote their own songs. Charles White claimed the distinction of having written at least forty of the greatest "Negro" song hits of his day, and perhaps less than ten per cent of the minstrel songs were genuinely Negro.

While "Jim Crow" and a few others of the earlier American song literature probably had an original Negro basis, many of the best known minstrel songs did not. Often African titles were given to songs with a clearly Caucasian theme and content. Every new song hit was parodied and imitated until only the expert investigator could find the original

[51] One of the best collections of this type of minstrel songs is *Schirmer's Household Series of Music Books, No. 35,—Negro Minstrel Melodies* (H. T. Burleigh, editor; preface by W. J. Henderson; New York, 1910).

version. A conventional Negro minstrel song type was rapidly established and the style imitated by scores of performers and composers. A writer in *Putnam's Monthly,* as early as 1855, deplored the fact that "poetasters who never saw an alligator or smelt the magnolia blossom in their lives sit coolly down to write an African ditty as a pleasant after-dinner pastime, or a daily task; and as a natural consequence of this reprehensible assumption, we find the banana growing wild in Tennessee, South Carolina slaves gorging themselves with pumpkin pie, a deceased Negress buried upon the St. Lawrence River in the midst of a furious snow, and a Kentucky sugar mill in full blast in the month of June."[52] The minstrels generally stressed the lighter side of the Negro's life, and some songs were definitely pro-planter and pro-Southern, and perhaps useful as propaganda. Professor White, in a collection of 680 Negro secular songs recently published by the Harvard University Press, claims to have found 104 "which contain such definite verbal echoes from the old minstrel songs as to leave no doubt as to the original home of the line or stanza concerned." It is the thesis of the writer that Negroes learned these songs from the white man, and after many repetitions, came to look upon them as their own. Since most of the famous collections of early minstrel

[52] Vol. V, 72-79, quoted in White, *American Negro Folksongs*, p. 9.

songs were out of print long before any significant number of Negroes had learned to read, these secular songs were handed down as part of the oral tradition of the Negro race in America. Indeed, some of these songs contain passages from several different minstrel favorites.[53]

It was the tradition of minstrelsy that the choruses of minstrel ballads be repeated several times by the quartette or the entire company, often in a kind of "lugubrious and under-the-breath whisper," a rendition supposed to be especially effective with audiences who loved close harmony. This device of humming or singing the chorus very softly during the repetition, was an immutable tradition of the first part. Some of the songs were extremely melancholy, others delightfully sprightly and gay. The balladists, in endless stanzas, bemoaned the passing of their sweethearts, or sang touchingly of the devotion of a mother watching in heaven over her wayward boy.

The theme of the song might range from "Just a Baby's Prayer at Twilight for a Daddy Over There" (a song used in the Field Minstrels during the Great War) through the whole repertory of sentimentalism about the "lone dank grave by the rippling river's side."[54] A balladist with Ordway's troupe was sing-

[53] See N. I. White, "The White Man in the Woodpile," and *American Negro Folk-Songs.*

[54] See Olive Logan, "The Ancestry of Brudder Bones," in *Harper's,* LVIII, 692.

ing a popular song in Boston in 1859 entitled, "Let me kiss him for his mother," the theme being derived from an incident which occurred in the South during a yellow fever epidemic.[55]  Audiences a generation or two ago during the Victorian age were thrilled and even wept over the plaintive lamentations of the minstrel boys about "Dearest May," "Poor Uncle Ned," "The Dandy Broadway Swell," "The Mellow Horn," "Camptown Races," "The Old Folks at Home," "the pastoral lays of the corn and cotton fields," and the songs of love and disappointment and death.  Audiences loved these melodies, according to one observer of American civilization, "for what it makes them forget and for what it makes them remember."[56]

It is easy to agree with the conclusion of perhaps the ablest modern student of Southern plantation life and its representation and distortion on the stage, that the song literature of America would really be impoverished "without the inevitable Swanee; happy levee scenes along the river shore; glorious moonlight that sleeps more sweetly on Southern banks than anywhere else; the gay girl of Dixie who may be white or black, tender or capricious, according to the mood of the composer, but

[55] *The New York Clipper*, March 5, 1859.
[56] Hiram Fuller, *Belle Brittan on Tour* (New York, 1858), pp. 334-336.

who is ever incomparable and irresistible; the darkey
frolic, specially the breakdown; the arms of mammy
and her crooning lullaby; a reminiscence of 'Ole
Massa,' or of 'Missy with her lovely silver hair';
the gustatory delights of chicken, 'possum or watermelon. . . ."[57] For the introduction and preserva-
tion of this element into American musical experience much credit must be given to the minstrel boys
of a generation or two ago.

Minstrel songs began to appear during the 1830's.
A decade earlier there were none to be found even
in the most complete collections of American popular
songs. "Daddy" Rice's "Jim Crow" became popular
all over the United States and Great Britain, with
many imitations and variations of the original version. "Old Zip Coon," "Long-Tailed Blue," "Set-
tin' on de Rail," "Ole Virginny Nebah Tire," Billy
Whitlock's "Lucy Long," "Clare de Kitchen," "Sich
a Gittin' up Stairs," and Dixon's "Coal Black Rose"
were famous before the close of "the fabulous forties." Indeed, during the political campaigns of that
stirring decade, numerous campaign jingles and
parodies were set to these well-known minstrel tunes.
"Zip Coon" and "Long Tail Blue" may have appeared on the variety stage as early as 1829. "Juba,"
a famous song with a clearly Caucasian theme, but
with an African title, was sung at Drury Lane The-

[57] Gaines, *op. cit.*, p. 141; see also his chapter on the development
of the conception of popular song (Chapter VI).

atre in London as early as 1816, and the Theatre
Royal of Dublin, in December, 1824, advertised
"Opossum up a gum tree" as a "real Negro
melody."[58]

"Zip Coon" has lived on under another name,
and "Turkey in the Straw," identical in tune, is still
the old fiddlers' delight.   In the original song, there
was a reference in one stanza to Generals Jackson
and Pakenham and the Battle of New Orleans, from
which it probably may be inferred that the song goes
back to early in the last century.  The opening
stanza was about

> Ole Zip Coon he is a larned skolar
> Sings 'posum up a gum tree an' coony in a holler.
> 'Posum up a gum tree, Coony on a stump,
> Den over dubble trubble, Zip Coon will jump.

In "Lucy Long," the listener learned that

> Miss Lucy she is handsome,
> And Miss Lucy she is tall,
> And de way she spreads her ankles,
> Is death to the niggers all.

Dan Emmett's "Old Dan Tucker" won a permanent place in American song books and the song
was widely used as a playparty game, and later re-
vived for a barn dance.   One of the most popular
stanzas related how

[58] N. I. White, "The White Man in the Woodpile," p. 210.

Old Dan Tucker was a fine old man,
Washed his face in a frying pan,
Combed his hair with a wagon wheel,
Died with the toothache in his heel.

"What's de Matter, Susey," as "composed and sung with unbounded applause by the original Old Dan Emmett" began as follows,

Sambo had a son born, he thought it was a daughter,
Yaller Sal de Georgia Stag, de big buck in de water.[59]

"Jim Along Jo" also was in great demand for a popular game played by sweethearts, and one finds it in use on various parts of the American frontier under names like "Hi, Come Along," "Fire on the Mountain," and "Jim Along Josie,"—the phrase "Jim Along" apparently being an imperative form of a verb meaning come or get along.[60] "Dandy Jim of Caroline," which tells the story of a conceited Negro's courting of "the lubly Dine" and ends with the christening of "eight or nine, Young Dandy Jims of Caroline," was introduced by the Kentucky Minstrels, probably as early as 1843.[61]

Some of these songs, like "Clare de Kitchen," remained popular for several decades. The reason must have been their musical jingle, for the words had little attractiveness. One stanza of "Clare de Kitchen" recounted how

[59] N. I. White, "The White Man in the Woodpile," p. 212.
[60] See Bruce E. Mahan and Pauline Grahame, "The Past at Play," in *The Palimpsest*, February, 1929.
[61] Brown, *History of the New York Stage*, I, 173.

A jay bird sat on a hickory limb,
He winked at me and I winked at him,
I picked up a stone and hit his shin,
Says he, "You better not do dat agin,"

while the chorus always repeated the figure,

Oh, clare de kitchen, old folks, young folks,
Clare de kitchen, old folks, young folks,
Ole Virginny neber tire.[62]

The same rollicking spirit appeared in a popular
stanza used by many of the early companies,

Now darkies sing and play and make a little fun,
We'll dance upon the green and beat the Congo drum,
We're a happy set of darkies, and we're assembled
    here to play,
So strike the bones and tambourine, and drive
    dull care away[63]

The Christy's introduced many of the earliest
minstrel songs, like "Young Clem Brown," "The
Colored Fancy Ball," "Walk in, Joe," "Rail Road
Trabeller," "My Skiff is by the Shore," "Car'lina,"
"Under de Shade ob de Old Gum Tree," "Virginia Juba," a nonsensical hodge podge in atrocious
rhythm, and "Goggle Tom," who "sweat like a lump
of roasted snow," sung to the tune of "Dandy Jim."
Sable Brothers' Minstrels featured "Faithless Fan"
and "Revolutionary Echoes," a patriotic and stir-

[62] Reprinted in E. T. Sawyer's, "Old Time Minstrels of San
Francisco," p. 5.
[63] Reprinted in Minnigerode, *op. cit.*, p. 232.

ring version of the days of '76, while Charley
White's Minstrels won great applause in their day
by such new favorites as "The Old Pine Tree,"
"The Dinner Horn," "Rosa's Wedding Day," and
"I'm Setting on de Rail, Dinah."   All of these songs
were popular before the close of the Civil War.

The "Rail Road Trabeller," a Christy favorite,
was a brief history of transportation and communi-
cation in America, with its many references to "de
steamboat" which "makes a mighty splutter," "de
hoss boat" which goes "so mighty slow," as contrasted with "de mail coach, good to cure de gout,
It will rattle off your buttons, and turn you inside
out"; and finally, "De telimagraph . . . good for
to transport the lightnen, Or to git the news from
Mexico, when the Yankees is a fitin'."   "Ole Bull
and Ole Dan Tucker," another Christy song, told in
rhymed couplets how Tucker defeated the famous
Norwegian violinist who toured the United States
in the 'fifties, in a battle between banjo and violin.

> Loud de banjo talked away,
> An' beat Ole Bull from de Norway,
> We'll take de shine from Paginini,
> We're de boys from ole Virginny.
>
> Ole Bull he made his elbow quiver,
> He played a shake and den a shiver;
> But when Dan Tucker touched his string,
> He'd make him shake like a locust's wing. . . .

In "Skiddy, Iddy, Di Do," the Christy's alluded, in timely fashion, to the Millerites, a sect which was making quite a disturbance in the religious life of the America of the middle period,

> Father Miller goes out preachin',
> About de world a comin' to pieces,
> Den if you want to do what's right,
> Just go and join de Millerite.

Campbell's Minstrels celebrated the virtues of the "Belle of Baltimore,"

> I've been through Carolina,
> I've been to Tennisse,
> I've trabelled Mississippi,
> For Massa set me free.
> I've kissed the lovely Creole,
> On Louisiana shore,
> But I've never found a gal to match
> De blooming Belle of Baltimore.[64]

Another favorite, "The Other Side of Jordan," began with a stanza about the banjo, and worked in many allusions to all the important events of the time, from the Crystal palace, the new Yankee clipper, *The Sovereign of the Seas,* the white slaves of England, and the "Bearded Lady" at P. T. Barnum's Museum, to the Hungarian revolutionist, Koszta, for whom an American Secretary of State had intervened so vigorously with the Austrian government in the 1850's.

[64] These and other songs of the period may be found in *Christy's Panorama Songster* (New York, n.d.).

"Walk in the Parlor," represented another type of minstrel song, and contained at least one stanza that had real merit,

> Lightning is a yaller gal, who libs up in de clouds,
> Thunder is a brack man, and he can holler loud,
> When he kisses Lightning, she darts up in a wonder,
> He jumps up and grabs de clouds and dat's what
>     makes it thunder.

In "Sally, Come Up," the audience learned that

> Sally has got a lubly nose,
> Flat across her face it grows,
> It sounds like t'under when it blows,
> Such a lubly nose has Sally.

"Stop Dat Knocking at My Door," a favorite of the Christy Minstrels, described the impetuous lover knocking at the door of his lady love, with "eyes so bright dey shine at night when de moon am gone away. . . ." "Going to the Silver Wedding" had a chorus devoted to the menu particularly appealing to darkies, and in "The Gum Tree Canoe," the minstrel crooned,

> All day in the field of soft cotton I hoe,
> I think of my Judy, and sing as I go.
> I caught her a bird with a wing of true blue,
> And at night rowed around in my gum-tree canoe.

"Josiphus Orange Blossom," a popular song with many disconnected and futile stanzas, in a reference to Civil War days, contained the phrase, a "red hot hunky dory contraband." The Christy's made the song so popular, that the American public adopted "hunky dory" as a part of their vocabulary. The stanzas of "Root, Hog, or Die," another favorite of the last century, on the other hand, are so utterly meaningless that it is difficult to understand how they became so popular throughout the country. In "The Little Octoroon," the brave old gunner took his love into his arms, while the chorus sang,

> 'Twas the loyal army sweeping to the sea,
> Flinging out the banner of the free,

and in "Billy's Dream," is found an amusing minstrel version of the Faust legend.

Before the 1850's, "The Gal from the South" was a favorite, and the song is found in many variations. It related how

> Ole Massa owned a colored girl—
> He bought her at the South;
> Her hair it curled so very tight,
> She could not shut her mouth.
> Her eyes they were so very small,
> They both ran into one,
> And when a fly lit in her eye,
> 'Twas like a June-bug in the sun.

The following song arose in the same period,

> Nigger's hair am berry short,
> White folks hair am longer,
> White folks dey smell very strong,
> Niggers dey smell stronger.

"The Big Sun Flower," Billy Emerson's great
song hit on the San Francisco minstrel stage, rhap-
sodized about the girl "with eyes as bright as evening stars," "so lovely and so shy." "Wake, Nicodemus" was written in a more serious vein, and was
almost a spiritual, with its touching reference to the
old Negro who wanted to be wakened in time for
the great, coming Jubilee, which was "long, long,
long on the way." The song closed with the stanza,

> There are signs in the sky that the darkness is gone
> There are tokens in endless array,
> While the storm which had seemingly banished the
>     dawn,
> Only hastens the advent of day.

Dick Carroll, in the days of Charley White's
Serenaders, sang

> We are from a place we don't know whar,
>     Ten miles from sea or land,
> We've trabled all this Continent
>     Wid dis our darky band.
>
> Our names are Julius, Clem an' Crow,
>     Wid Erastus and his brudder;
> We all belong to one family,
>     But neber seen our mudder.[65]

Finally, in "Ham's Banjo," the story of the
origin of this famous instrument is told in musical
form. The song began,

[65] Charles H. Day, *Fun in Black*, p. 35.

> Go way fiddle! folks is tired hearing you squawkin'
> Keep silent for your betters—don't you hear de
>      banjo talkin'?

The tale of confusion on Noah's Ark then was re-
told in Negro verse, as a preliminary to Ham's in-
vention of the banjo, on which he played, as his first
tune, "Never Mind the Weather."

> Now Ham, de only nigger dat was runnin' on de
>      packet,
> Got lonesome in de barbershop and couldn't stand
>      de racket,
> So for to amuse himself he steamed some wood
>      and bent it,
> An' soon he had a banjo made, de first dat was
>      invented.

From that day to this, "Where you find de nigger,
dere's a banjo and de possum."[66]

By 1870, Christy had issued half a dozen collections of plantation melodies, and other minstrel
performers and managers published many volumes
of popular music. It was not long until these songs
appeared in all collections of music found in almost
every well-ordered American household of the last
century, and in this way minstrelsy made its contribution to the musical heritage of the American peo-

[66] Reprinted in Al G. Field, "History of American Minstrelsy," in
*The Kit Kat*, VIII, 60-61.

ple.[67] Even many western ballads were sung to tunes made popular by the minstrels. When the Civil War veterans returned from the South, they brought with them still another addition to the American "Song-bag," namely the "jubilee" songs which expressed the Negro's happiness and excitement over his new-won freedom. It was a far-cry from these songs to the ragtime, "blues," and jazz of later days, but minstrel endmen made it their business to keep abreast of the developing tastes of their audiences.

[67] Among many collections, the following may be mentioned: William F. Allen, *Slave Songs of the United States* (New York, 1867); William E. Barton, *Old Plantation Hymns* (Boston, 1899); H. T. Burleigh; *Negro Minstrel Melodies* (New York, 1910), and *Plantation Melodies; Old and New* (New York, 1901); *Wood's New Plantation Melodies* (New York, 18—); *George Christy and Wood's Melodies as sung by their unique company at Minstrel Hall, 444 Broadway, N. Y.* (New York, 1854), and *Christy's Panorama Songster; containing the songs sung by Christy, Campbell, Pierce's Minstrels, and Sable Brothers* (New York, 1860); Charles H. Fox, *Sable Songster* (Philadelphia, 1859) and *Ethiopian Songster* (Philadelphia, 1858); George Harrington, *Christy's and White's Ethiopian Melodies* (Philadelphia, 1854); Elias Howe, Jr. *Ethiopian Glee Book* (Boston, 1849); *Minstrel Songs Old and New. A Collection of world-wide famous minstrel and plantation songs including the celebrated Foster melodies with pianoforte accompaniment* (Boston, 1882); *The Negro Forget-me-not Songster* (Philadelphia, 18—); and *Nigger Melodies; being the only entire and complete work of Ethiopian Songs extant* (New York, 18—); *Old Plantation Songster* (Philadelphia, 18—) and *Uncle Ned Songster* (Philadelphia, 18—); *Uncle True, Songster* (Fisher and Brothers, Philadelphia, 18—); Charles White, *White's New Ethiopian Song Book* (Philadelphia, 18—) and *White's new illustrated Melodeon Song Book* (New York, 1848); *Pop, goes the Weasel, songster* (Philadelphia, 18—); and *Billy Birch's Ethiopian Melodist* (New York, 1862). Numerous old minstrel songs in sheet form can be found in the collection of the Grosvenor Library in Buffalo.

By their desire to give the public what was new, they gradually got further and further away from the plantation music from which their art had sprung.[68]

Even before the close of the Civil War, the end-men began to perform songs that had little or no connection with Negro themes, and were intended merely to be funny. George Christy's collection, *Essence of Old Virginny,* issued in 1864, for example, contained a song about the man who married sixteen wives, with these ridiculous lines,

> For polygamy's arrested;
> A boy has swallowed nine clasp-knives,
> And all of them digested;
> A cat has hatched young ducklings two
> Each one frisks and capers;
> They're both alive—it must be true
> Because it's in the papers.[69]

Another popular Christy song referred to the craze for patents,

> There's patent physic for the sick,
> Though some will be found scoffing,
> And die, just to enjoy the sweets,
> Of a snug, patent coffin;
> We've patent pills and powders too,
> That's sure to cure or kill 'em;
> Besides, we've patent cradles, and
> We've patent means to fill 'em.

[68] See Gaines, *op. cit.,* pp. 134-137. Many of the songs referred to in the preceding pages can be conveniently found, with the tune and piano accompaniment, in Paskman and Spaeth, *op. cit.,* pp. 38-50, 74-75, 51-57, 64-69, 204-208.

[69] Pp. 66-67.

To the tune of "The Girl I Left Behind Me,"
Christy sang "The Duel,"

> Big Mr. Knott, and Mr. Schott,
> Three glorious rounds they fought;
> When Mr. Knott, he got the shot,
> And Schott, he got it not;
> So Knott was shot, and Schott was not,
> And Schott the glory got.[70]

Many black face singers also sang songs in "Dutch
dialect," around the middle of the last century, when
the German immigration to the United States was
very heavy.[71]

The oil boom in Pennsylvania, in the early 'sixties, prompted the Christy Minstrels to inflict the
song, "Striking Ile" on the public who learned how

> The world revolves on its own axle-tree,
> Once in twenty-four hours, says G. O. Graffee;
> The axle got hot, and the world stopt awhile,
> And the people have all gone to "boring for ile."[72]

To the tune of "Central Park of a Sunday
Night," the endmen of Christy's organization sang
a comic parody in which many of the great figures
of the Civil War era passed in quick review—Andy
Johnson, who "each night goes sober to bed"; Secretary of the Navy, Welles, "on gunboats daft";
Charley Sumner, "making niggers lawyers every

---

[70] Christy's *Bones and Banjo Melodist*, pp. 39-40.
[71] *Ibid.*, pp. 15-16.
[72] *Ibid.*, pp. 65-66.

day"; shoddy-merchants trying to cheat the country; Benjamin F. Butler, "talking many a lie"; Stanton, General Dix, Seward, Thurlow Weed, and army generals, "not at the front, but on the spree."[73]

Medleys also were very popular with minstrel audiences. These were constructed by a process of wholesale borrowing from perhaps a score of well-known songs. One illustration will suffice, "The Song of Songs," as sung by the Christy Minstrels in the 1860's.

> I dreamt I dwelt in marble halls,
>   With the dark gal dressed in blue;
> And didn't she seem to like it,
>   When early falls the dew. . . .
>
> .    .    .    .    .
>
> Come into the garden, Maud,
>   Underneath the willow tree!
> In such a moment I'll but ask,
>   That you'll remember me!
> Let me like a soldier fall,
>   In a garret near the sky;
> Troubadour enchanting,
>   Beef, pork, mutton, will you buy? . . .
>
> .    .    .    .    .
>
> Then take this cup of sparkling wine,
>   There is some one knocking at the door.
> If you'll lull this tempest of the heart,
>   I'll ask for nothing more.[74]

The ballads of American minstrel shows ran the whole gamut of human emotions and sentimental

[73] Christy's *Bones and Banjo Melodist*, pp. 58-59.
[74] *Ibid.*, pp. 61-62.

unrestraint.   Fred Buckley, one of the earliest performers, with the Virginia Minstrels, composed
some of the first minstrel ballads, sentimental songs
like, "We Are Growing Old Together," "I See Her
Still in My Dreams," and "I'm Turning Gray, Dear
Kate."[75]

James Powers, a song writer during the middle
of the last century, wrote, "She Sleeps in the Grave,"
and "Faded Flowers," lachrimose effusions that
once enjoyed great favor with the public.   In
*Christy's Panorama Songster,* there appeared
"Mary's Grave," a composition by a certain H. Wilson, who wrote,

On a lone barren shore war de wild roaring billow,
Beat hard on de beach, and de loud winds do rave,
My Mary lies still wid de earth for a pillow,    :
And fond weeping Pompey leans ober her grave!

It was a tragic tale, the story of Mary's death, and
occasionally she returned to haunt her faithless
lover,

. . . Last night in my cabin, when it rain'd and it thunder,
So dark war de heavens, so black war de sky,
De floor it did open and Mary rose up dar,
She look in my face and she dese words did say,
Weep, Pompey, weep, for by your jealous deeds see,
My death you have caused, but now you are free.[76]

[75] Rice, *Monarchs of Minstrelsy,* pp. 10-18.
[76] P. 131.

Neil Price, a minstrel who died in 1889, gave the
American public the touching ballad, "A Boy's Best
Friend Is His Mother." The noted basso, Charles
F. Shattuck, not content to startle his hearers by his
lower register as revealed in old time favorites like
"Rocked in the Cradle of the Deep," composed "One
Hundred Fathoms Deep."[77]   W. S. Mullally, a per-
former during the last half of the nineteenth cen-
tury, wrote "Mottoes That Are Framed upon the
Wall," while Dan E. Lyons composed the popular
song of a generation ago, "It's a Long Lane That
Has No Turn."[78]

Of the same vintage were favorites like "Al-
ways Take Mother's Advice," "The Letter That
Never Came," "A Violet from Mother's Grave,"
"The Picture That Was Turned Toward the Wall,"
"A Lock of My Mother's Hair," and "Found Dead
in the Snow." Songs like "The Old Oaken Bucket,"
"Silver Threads Among the Gold," and "Seeing
Nellie Home" survived the ravages of time and still
grace American collections of the "Hundred Best
Songs." "When You and I Were Young, Maggie,"
was sung with great success in the 1870's, and remained a favorite to the present day.   Jack Richards,
baritone soloist with the Al G. Field Minstrels and
one of the greatest singers in the history of the minstrel stage, continued to sing the song with remark-

[77] Rice, *Monarchs of Minstrelsy*, pp. 51, 90, 140.
[78] *Ibid.*, p. 178.

able success on the vaudeville stage after leaving this minstrel organization.    Billy Emerson sang "Love Among the Roses" with unusual success in the days when the San Francisco Minstrels were famous. Benjamin Russell Hanby, an alumnus of Otterbein College, at Westerville, Ohio, wrote "Darling Nelly Gray," and later tried in vain to repeat his success with new songs like "Little Tillie's Grave."[79]    Another song to be compared with "Darling Nellie Gray," was the well-known "Elsie Lee."

> Where the little old Appomattox
> Wash along its sandy shore;
> Where the nightingales are singing sweet to me.
> Through these scenes I seem to wander,
> As in days of long ago
> When I courted my own darling Elsie Lee.

M. B. Leavitt wrote a long list of sentimental ballads, published by Oliver Ditson, including, "Little Footsteps," "The Cot Where the Old Folks Died," "We Miss Thee from Our Cottage Home," "Yes, I Will Write Thee from Home," "Put My Little Shoes Away," and "The Little Grave Under the Willow."[80]    Songs like "Would I Were a Boy Again" and "Come, Dwell With Me" were popular as early as the 1850's.[81]

[79] See C. B. Galbreath, "Song Writers of Ohio," in the *Ohio Archaeological and Historical Quarterly*, XIV, 180-215.

[80] Leavitt, *op. cit.*, p. 147.

[81] *The New York Clipper*, September 29, 1877.

In the late 1890's, "When the Little Ones Are Coming Home from School," by Charles Graham, and John T. Kelly's ballad, "We Were Sweethearts, Nellie and I" were great favorites on minstrel programs.[82] In the same period, "Honey Boy" Evans' songs, "I'll Be True to My Honey Boy," and "Standing on the Corner, Didn't Mean No Harm," swept the country.[83] The same composer gave Americans "In the Good Old Summertime." In 1902, Eddie Leonard, appearing with Primrose and Dockstader's Minstrels, introduced "I'm So Tired of Livin' I Don't Care When I Die." The assassination of President McKinley and the Spanish-American War were responsible for such musical·atrocities as "The Doom of Anarchy," and "All Honor to Admiral Schley."[84]

In the ballad singing age of the last century, when young men and women met around the pianoforte at stated evenings each week "and pursued one another vocally" through the intricate repetitions of their favorites, many songs fairly dripped with the sentimentality or morality of the period. One of the favorites of the 'forties was a discourse on virtue,

> Virtue, my Emma, is a gem,
> The mind's pellucid diadem,
> To fellow mortals kindly given,
> A foretaste of a type of Heaven;

[82] *The New York Clipper*, January 4, 1896, March 14, 1896.
[83] *Ibid.*, February 22, 1896.
[84] *Ibid.*, November 1, 1901.

> Pure and White as mountain snow
> That hurries to the vale below,
> Yet genial as the glorious sun
> Which makes it unpolluted run—
> Which makes it—
> Makes it unpolluted run—
> Which makes it unpolluted run."

Simpering maidens learned that

> Love can ne'er be forced to tarry,
> Chain him, he'll the bonds remove;
> Paired, not matched, too many marry,
> All should wed alone for love. . . .

But in spite of eloquent musical admonitions about morality and prudence, one of the most popular songs of the 'forties was, "I Was Not to Blame, Mother."

> Oft hast thou told me, Mother dear,
> Subtle man I'd cause to fear—
> Thou a saint in yonder skies
> Still thy warning voice I prize;
> But if he would still pursue,
> Mother dear, what could I do?
> Let this little tear proclaim,
> Mother, I was not to blame. . . .

It was an age when

> Hands our cruel sires united,
> Hearts were deemed to slight avail;
> Thus my youth's bright morn o'erclouded,
> Thus betrothed to wealth and state;
> All love's own sweet prospect shrouded,
> I have found thee, but too late. . . .[85]

[85] These stanzas are reprinted in Minnigerode, *op. cit.*, pp. 236-237, 238, 242, 244.

In Christy's Minstrels, "No One to Love" proved a very popular ballad throughout the decade of the 'sixties. Through many stanzas, the singer wailed that there was

> No one to love, none to caress,
> Roaming alone through this world's wilderness,

and ended with a tremendous sigh for the "mansions above."[86]

In the same decade, suffering, unhappy humanity was advised by minstrel balladists to

> Love not! Love not! ye helpless sons of clay,
> Hope's gayest wreaths are made of earthly flowers,
> Things that are made to fade and fall away,
> Ere they have blossom'd for a few short hours.
>
> .     .     .     .     .
>
> Love not! Love not! the thing you love may die,
> May perish from the gay and gladsome earth,
> The silent stars, the blue and smiling sky,
> Beams on its grave, as once upon its birth.[87]

Harry Howard, a member of the Christy Company, sang "She Hath Gone," one of the most lugubrious bits of sentimental trash that Christy's Opera House in Chicago ever released on the American public.

> She hath gone in the spring time of life,
> When the young heart was buoyant and light
> Ere earth with its sorrowing strife
> Had cast o'er her spirit a blight.

[86] *George Christy's Essence of Old Kentucky*, p. 23.
[87] *Christy's Panorama Songster*, p. 137.

She was wandering with hope through the bowers,
Where her footsteps delighted to stray;
But the spoiler had looked 'mid the flowers,
And she passed in her gladness away. . . .

. . . . . .

She hath gone from a world where the thorn
Is concealed 'neath the breast of the rose,
Where the skies which are brightest at morn,
Will darken in gloom ere the close.

And in "My Poor Lost Nell," as sung by D. Meldum of the same company, the minstrel pleaded,

Oh lay me in the same dear spot,
Where lies my poor lost Nell;
'Tis near the well-remembered cot,
'Neath the willow in the dell.

and presently we learn that "Poor Lost Nell" was out riding horse-back, when a bolt of lightning frightened her otherwise trusty steed, the animal ran away, and the helpless rider was drowned in a roaring stream.[88]

But not all the songs of minstrelsy were of this depressing sort. Minstrel song books were full of comic ditties, like "All That Glitters Is Not Gold," "Bitter Beer," "Courting in the Rain," "Casey's Whiskey," "Danny Takes After His Father," "Fie, for Shame; or What Will Mamma Say," "It's Not the Miles We Travel, But the Pace," and "You Never Miss the Water Till the Well Runs Dry." Irish

[88] Christy's *Bones and Banjo Melodist*, pp. 5-6, 33.

songs, like "Home Rule for Ireland for Evermore," "The Irish Regiment," and "Land of Saint Patrick" were popular with minstrel audiences, which always contained numerous Irish-Americans who had but recently come to the United States as immigrants. In the 1860's, the Christy Minstrels sang "The Bonny Green Flag," to the tune of "Sprig of Shillelagh," concluding with the stanza,

> Here's to the bonny green flag, and long may it wave,
> With the stars and stripes in the land of the brave,
> And at no distant day, it will once more float free,
> On that dear little Island over the sea. . . .[89]

One of many minstrel parodies on "Comin' Thro' the Rye," was entitled "Kissing on the Sly," and ran as follows,

> His manly whisker swept her cheek
>   She uttered no reply;
> How could she part her lips to speak,
>   While kissing on the sly?
> There's such a sum of smacking bliss,
>   That Croesus could not buy,
> The honeyed worth of one sweet kiss,
>   That's taken on the sly.[90]

Toward the close of the last century, the modern "coon songs" became popular on the minstrel stage.

[89] Christy's *Bones and Banjo Melodist*, p. 55. For other examples, see also Ed. James, *op. cit.*

[90] *Ibid.*, p. 18. For other interesting specimens of the songs of our fathers and grandfathers see the excellent collections of Sigmund Spaeth, *Read 'Em and Weep* (Garden City, 1926) and *Weep Some More My Lady* (Garden City, 1927).

It was in the 1890's, that the ragtime melodies of Ernest Hogan, Harry von Tilzer, May Irwin, Cole and Johnson flourished.  Harry von Tilzer's

> Rufus Rastus Johnson Brown,
> What you gonna do when the rent comes round,
>
> Coon, coon, coon, I wish my color would fade,
> Coon, coon, coon, I like a brighter shade,

will be remembered as popular minstrel songs early in the present century.  More recently, the "blues" have superseded the "coon songs" of several decades ago.

A few of the minstrel songs were destined to endure.  One was the still popular "Carry Me Back to Old Virginny," introduced to American audiences as early as 1845 by Sanford, with the Virginia Minstrels in Philadelphia.[91]  "The Days of '49" apparently was written by Charles Roads, one of the early banjo players on the Pacific coast, who began his career as a singer in the mining camps of California, and later was a member of many minstrel companies.  The song was typical of the mining frontier, and has lived as one of the musical survivals of the romantic days of the gold rush.  In the first stanza, the song introduced

> . . . Kentucky Bill, one of the boys,
> Who was always in for a game.
> No matter whether he lost or won,

[91] Wright, *Hawkers and Walkers*, p. 188.

To him 'twas all the same;
He'd ante a slug, he'd pass the buck,
He'd go a hatful blind;
In a game with death Bill lost his breath
In the days of '49.[92]

It was E. P. Christy's minstrel performers who introduced the songs of Stephen C. Foster to the American public, although many years passed before Foster's compositions received the recognition they deserved. Indeed, it may be said that Negro minstrelsy, born in a northern theatre, prepared the way for America's appreciation of Foster, and later, of Uncle Remus. E. P. Christy himself, who performed to banjo accompaniment, was among the first to sing "My Old Kentucky Home," "Massa's in de Cold, Cold Ground," and "Old Black Joe."

Foster was born in Pittsburgh, in 1826. What formal education he had was received at Athens Academy and Jefferson College, Pennsylvania. His father was a native of Virginia who had risen to some prominence in Pennsylvania, as is evidenced by the fact that he held some minor political offices in that state. The boy Stephen was for a time under the care of a mulatto nurse who happened to be an expert dancer. Later on, he lived in Cincinnati, and made numerous trips up and down the Ohio and the Mississippi. In 1843, a Pittsburgh confectioner with a flair for minstrelsy and money which he was will-

[92] E. T. Sawyer, "Old Time Minstrels in San Francisco," p. 7.

ing to spend to encourage the development of this type of entertainment, offered a prize for the best original Negro song. Foster submitted a composition entitled "Way Down South, Whar de Corn Grows," but did not receive the award. Not discouraged, he continued to compose songs of this kind. First came "Louisiana Belle," "Uncle Ned," and "O Susanna" and then, in rather rapid succession, his better known compositions, "Nelly Was a Lady" (1849), "My Old Kentucky Home," "Camptown Races" (1850), and "Old Folks at Home" (1851). The last became so popular that Christy paid five hundred dollars for the privilege of having his name printed as an advertisement on the title page, and the royalties from this composition reached fifteen thousand dollars. It is interesting to note in passing that according to one account Foster originally intended to use the Yazoo for the "Suwanee River" in this composition. According to another account, "Suwanee Ribber" was the Negro corruption of San Juan, the Spanish name for St. John's River in Florida. There followed "Massa's in the Cold Ground" (1852), "O Boys, Carry Me 'Long" (1853), "Hard Times Come Again No More" (1854), "Way Down South" and "Old Lemuel" (1858), and "Old Black Joe" (1860). Besides these well-known songs, Foster also wrote a great many sentimental ballads to satisfy the demand of the times for this kind of music, like "Ah, May the Red Rose Live Always," "Jennie With the Light-Brown Hair," "I See Her Still in My Dreams," and "Come Where My Love Lies Dreaming." Foster's mother died in 1861, and this tragedy may have inspired many of the composer's later songs.

Foster's melodies were popular for decades on the minstrel stage and in the concert halls. Through the traveling minstrel companies, and especially through the River Boat minstrels who went up and down the Mississippi and its more important tributaries, they were carried to all parts of the United States. Foster died in January, 1864, at the early age of thirty-eight, unhonored, but not unsung. The real greatness of his art, its simplicity, its universal appeal, and its emotional richness intended to express the joys and sorrows of the southern slave population,—qualities which have made his songs part of the meager stock of American folkmusic—were not fully appreciated until years after Foster's death.[98] It was the minstrel stage which prompted Foster to write some of his best compositions, and it was the minstrel performers who introduced them to the American public.

There is some evidence to show that "The

[98] See J. G. Burnett, "National Elements in Stephen Foster's Art," in *South Atlantic Quarterly*, XXI, 322-326; and Robert Nevin, "Stephen C. Foster and Negro Minstrelsy," in *Atlantic Monthly*, XX, 608-616.

Bonnie Blue Flag," the popular war song of the South; "Tramp, Tramp, Tramp, the Boys are Marching"; and "Tenting on the Old Camp Ground," all famous Civil War songs, were first heard on the minstrel stage.[94] This is certainly true of "Dixie," once the war song of a Lost Cause, and today one of the nation's most popular patriotic airs. "Dixie" is minstrelsy's permanent contribution to American patriotic music.

"Dixie" or "Dixie's Land," as it was originally named, was the creation of Daniel Decatur Emmett, one of the original "Big Four" who organized the Virginia Minstrels in the early 1840's. In 1857, Emmett was engaged by Bryant's Minstrels, then playing at 470 Broadway, New York, as a musician and composer of Negro songs and plantation "walk-arounds." On a Saturday in 1859, the owner of the show asked Emmett to write a "hooray song" or "walk-around" in time for Monday's rehearsal. He was instructed to produce a specially catchy tune, the words were of minor importance. According to the generally accepted story, Emmett took up his violin on a dreary, rainy, Sunday morning, and struggled vainly for a tune. As he looked out of the window, upon the depressing scene outside, he sighed, "I wish I were in Dixie," a phrase often used by showmen in the winter time, and with which Em-

[94] Leavitt, *op. cit.*, pp. 30-31, 60.

mett was familiar because of his experiences in the
South with circuses. He began to hum these words
and to improvise a tune on his violin. After com-
pleting the melody, he wrote the words, and on
Monday morning, the copy was ready in time for
rehearsal. The music was not changed, but the first
stanza which, it was believed, might offend some religious people if the song should ever appear as sheet
music, was deleted. The questionable stanza ran as
follows,

> Dis worl' was made in jiss six days,
> An' finished up in various ways;
>     Look away! look away! look away! Dixie Land.
> Dey den made Dixie trim an' nice,
> But Adam call'd it "Paradise."
>     Look away! look away! look away! Dixie Land.

By this omission, what was originally intended for
the second stanza of the song became the first. The
chorus remained unchanged. Stanzas were added
from time to time until there were a score or more,
but almost all were reminiscent of "the land of cotton" with "cinnamon seas and sandy bottoms." The
original song appears in many collections with many
variations.[95]

"Dixie" was used first as the "walk-around" for
Bryant's Minstrels and the song became rather well
known in the North. There is some evidence to show
that it was used in 1860 by the Republican party as

[95] For various versions, see C. B. Galbreath, *Daniel Decatur Emmett*, pp. 13, 14-19.

a campaign song, but with different words to fit the needs of Lincoln's campaign for the presidency. The song was issued by a sheet music publisher, apparently without the consent of the author, who later on was offered five dollars for his copyright by a Southern publisher.

In 1861 "Dixie" became the war song of the South. There has been some effort made to establish the fact that Emmett himself sang the song in Montgomery, Alabama, in 1859,[96] but according to the generally accepted version, "Dixie" was introduced to the South by Mrs. John Wood, an actress playing burlesque in New Orleans just before the outbreak of hostilities in the Civil War. In John Brougham's production of *Pocohontas,* which was the attraction at the New Orleans Varieties Theatre, the manager decided to add a drill and march of forty female Zouaves, in order to make the presentation more attractive to his audiences. Carlo Patti, a brother of the famous Adelina, was the leader of the orchestra, and after experimenting with several airs, he selected "Dixie" as the tune for the proposed drill. That night the female Zouaves marched on the stage, singing "I wish I was in Dixie." The melody captured the audience, seven encores were demanded and soon the tune was being whistled in the streets of New Orleans as a musical

[93] Al G. Field, *Watch Yourself Go By,* p. 532.

sensation. When the Civil War broke out, "Dixie" was arranged as a quickstep for the Confederate regiments from Louisiana, and thus found its way into the Confederate ranks. According to one account, on July 4, 1861, while the Confederates were drawn up in Virginia within hearing distance of the federal cannon booming a national salute, General Kirby Smith reported that his men had no powder to waste on salutes, "but our bands played 'Dixie' from one end of the line to the other."[97] Before long, the "walk-around," written by a Northern man for a New York minstrel show, was accepted throughout the South as the war song of the Confederacy.[98] Notwithstanding the song's great popularity, Emmett realized only five hundred dollars from his copyright.

After Emmett's death, a correspondent of the Baltimore Sun claimed that Harry McCarthy, an Arkansas comedian who died in 1874 and who was the reputed author of "The Bonnie Blue Flag," had written "Dixie" also, but the records of the United States copyright office and of music publishers seem to substantiate Emmett's claims to this distinction.[99]

[97] The South in the Building of the Nation (Southern Publication Society, 1909), VII, 68.

[98] See Galbreath, op. cit., pp. 12-21; 26-27; 28; 31-36; 38-40; Brander Matthews, op. cit., p. 755; and Mary C. Owens, Memories of the Professional and Social Life of John E. Owens, by his Wife (Baltimore, 1892), pp. 110-111.

[99] For a detailed discussion of this controversy, see Galbreath, op. cit., pp. 31-36, 38-40.

It is certain, however, that many other "Dixie" songs were written, especially during the Civil War, and set to Emmett's melody, sometimes with the author's consent, and often without his knowledge. Although many variations of the stanzas of "Dixie" are in existence, few of these imitations made any significant changes in the chorus Emmett had composed.

Lincoln, who was very fond of Negro minstrelsy, and revelled in its crude jokes and slap-stick comedy, seems to have been specially pleased by "Dixie." In 1860, about two months before his nomination for the presidency, he was in Chicago attending the sessions of the United States Court, as attorney for the Illinois Central Railroad, in the famous "Sand Bar" litigation, involving title to land along the lake front. With his friend, Henry C. Whitney, Lincoln attended a performance of Rumsey and Newcomb's Minstrels. Here he heard "Dixie," probably for the first time. According to Whitney's account, he applauded violently, and shouted, "Let's have it again! Let's have it again!" Within a year this rollicking "walk-around" had become the battle-cry of half of a disrupted nation.[100]

[100] See Jesse W. Weik, *The Real Lincoln* (Boston, 1923), pp. 75, 85-86; and Albert J. Beveridge, *Abraham Lincoln* (Boston, 1928), I, 536, 597-598.

# CHAPTER V

## KNIGHTS OF THE BURNT CORK

A long line of minstrel kings have come and gone, and have left hardly a trace which the historian might seize upon in his efforts to save these unique American entertainers from total oblivion. Their names appear on the old playbills; we know a little of the programs they presented, but in only a few cases enough to reconstruct a brief biographical note about their careers. Very little is known of even the more prominent performers, like Milt Barlow, Lew Benedict, the three Rankins, Luke Schoolcraft and his partner, Coes, Sam Sharpley, the two Westons, Dick José, Barney Fagan, Frank McNish, Carroll Johnson, Chuck Atkinson, the peerless bone player, Pete Lee, Sam Devere, Bob Hart, Newcomb, Shorey, Duprez, and hundreds of others.[1] George Washington Dixon, "Dummy" Allen and "Daddy" Rice always will be remembered as the pioneers of minstrelsy, but comparatively little has been recorded about their careers. The discussion of the career and work of individual minstrels to which this chapter is devoted, cannot pretend to do more than make a random selection of a few of the blackface artists whose names, at least, have

[1] See a poem, "A Song of Minstrel Men," in *Stage and Foyer*, March, 1926, p. 12.

been preserved. Hundreds of minstrels, some probably of major importance in the development of the technique of their art, must be passed over without comment, for in their cases, the record is silent.

Fortunately, quite a little is known about the interesting career of Daniel Decatur Emmett, one of the original "Big Four," and for decades one of the best known figures on the minstrel stage. Emmett was born in Mt. Vernon, Ohio, on October 29, 1815. He came from Irish stock, and his forbears were Virginia pioneers who had yielded to the call of the western wilderness and, with others of their kind, had crossed the Blue Ridge, and entered Ohio by way of Wheeling. Emmett's grandfather was a veteran of the Revolution, and his father, as a volunteer in the War of 1812 in the regiment of Lewis Cass, participated in the important engagements of Fort Meigs and Detroit. The minstrel's brother became a chief justice of the Supreme Court of Minnesota.

Dan Emmett received only the most elementary education. As a lad, he worked in the newspaper offices of the Norwalk, Ohio, *Huron Reflector,* and the *Western Aurora,* published in his home town. He seems to have had a special gift for music. "Old Dan Tucker," one of his best known songs, was composed at Mt. Vernon when he was not over sixteen years of age. At seventeen, he enlisted in the United

States Army as a fifer, and served at various posts in Kentucky and Missouri. After leaving the army, Emmett traveled with circus bands. It was in the early 'forties, as has been related elsewhere, that he organized the Virginia Minstrels, generally considered the first Negro minstrel troupe in the United States. Emmett apparently was a good singer, as well as a skillful performer on many instruments, especially the violin and the flute. His musical compositions range all the way from sentimental ballads to "break-downs," jigs, and reels. After returning from Europe, following the disbanding of the Virginia Minstrels, Emmett traveled for a time as a circus musician. In 1857, he joined Bryant's Minstrels in New York, and served that company as a musician, singer, and composer until the close of the Civil War. It was while a member of this company that he wrote "Dixie," the song that was to win him everlasting fame. During the Civil War, Emmett was a strong Union Democrat.

At various times during his career, he played with White's and Leavitt's companies, and for a time, he had his own company on the road. From the close of the Civil War to 1888, Emmett's official residence was in Chicago. Then he returned to the town of his birth, where he lived in comparative obscurity among the farmers and townsmen of Mt. Vernon, until Al G. Field, whom Emmett had befriended in the 1870's while managing a concert hall in Chicago, decided to bring "Uncle Dan" out of his retirement and back to the burnt cork circle. In the summer of 1895, Emmett began his tour of the country as a member of the Field Minstrels. His first appearance was at Newark, Ohio. Field had planned merely to introduce the old star as the "father of American minstrelsy," while the orchestra played "Dixie," but Uncle Dan insisted upon singing the song, although over thirty-five years had elapsed since he had given "Dixie" to an American audience in New York, and over twenty-one years since his last appearance on a minstrel stage. Emmett followed his song with a few remarks, announcing his farewell tour. This procedure was observed wherever the show played. In the South, Emmett received ovation after ovation, and was lavishly entertained. When the season closed at Ironton, Ohio, April 11, 1896, Emmett returned to Mt. Vernon, where he received sufficient funds from the sale of autographed copies of "Dixie" and benefits from the Actors' Fund of New York to enable him to live without want. In 1902, Emmett appeared once more in a local performance of the Elks Lodge of Mt. Vernon, and the tears coursed down his cheeks when the audience rose as he walked across the stage to sing "Dixie" for the last time. Emmett died at Mt. Vernon, on June 28, 1904, after a very brief illness. In accordance with his wish, he was buried by the local lodge of Elks, under the direction of Al G. Field. As his coffin was slowly lowered into the new-made grave, the strains of "Dixie," played by a band, floated out upon the evening air.

Emmett always will be remembered as the composer of "Dixie." But he wrote many other songs, literally hundreds, which enjoyed their brief span of popularity. Of many of these songs the composer himself did not even keep a copy. "Jordan is a Hard Road to Travel," "Here We Are, or Cross ober Jordan," "Road to Richmond," "Black Brigade," "Billy Patterson," "Dar's a Darkey in De Tent," "Mac (General George B. McClellan) Will Win the Union Back," and many other forgotten favorites, came from the pen of Uncle Dan. He also left many instrumental compositions, a "Standard Drummer," a collection of Negro sermons, some songs written in Irish brogue, in one of the best of which, "The Offish Saiker," he advised "Turn ivry foiriner out, an' put the Irish in!", and some farces, among which was "Hard Times," written in 1854, and the only one to win any recognition. Emmett also left a whole manuscript volume of "walk-arounds."[2]

Much less is known about the other members of

[2] The best biographical sketch of Emmett is Charles Burleigh Galbreath, *Daniel Decatur Emmett*. This little volume also contains many of Emmett's songs. I have followed Galbreath in the main in presenting this brief account of Emmett's activities.

the original "Big Four." Billy Whitlock was born in 1813, and worked as a typesetter on the *New York Herald.* After his minstrel experience, he appeared for a time with Barnum's Circus. He also is remembered as the composer of "Lucy Long." Whitlock died in 1878. Dick Pelham (1815-1876) and Frank Brower (1820-1874) were mainly song and dance men. The former played in "Oh Hush," as early as 1835; the latter, besides his minstrel engagements, played in various museum shows and circuses. Brower, popularly known as "Uncle Frank," visited England in 1851, where he played as a clown in a circus. After his retirement from the stage in 1867, he became a saloon-keeper in Philadelphia.[3]

Edwin P. Christy, organizer of the first Christy Minstrels, began life as office boy for a New York lawyer. Later, he worked as a hotel clerk and traveling shoe salesman. With his meager savings, he organized his first company of three or four performers in Buffalo. Within twelve years, he was able to retire with sufficient earnings to live in comfort. He had two sons who also entered the profession, but they died in their twenties. One son, William E., was a successful comedian and endman, especially good in female impersonations; the other, E. Byron, was known for his witty stump speeches.

[3] See Brown, *History of the American Stage,* and Rice, *Monarchs of Minstrelsy,* p. 12.

Christy himself committed suicide in 1862, when, in a temporary fit of insanity, he leaped from the second story of his New York residence.  Much of the credit for minstrelsy's rapid rise to popularity must be given to the managerial skill of E. P. Christy.[4]

George N. Christy, whose real name was Harrington, took E. P. Christy's name when as a mere lad he began his career as a jig dancer in the Christy show.   Harrington was born at Palmyro, New York, November 3, 1827.  He became famous as a comedian and mimic, and as a successful manager. He was especially well known as a female impersonator, and introduced the "Negro wench" characterization to minstrelsy.  He died in 1868, of inflammation of the brain.

Luke West, whose real name was William Sheppard, probably was the first to introduce whistling solos into a minstrel program.  This was in 1845, in Hoboken.  He played at various times with Campbell's Minstrels and the Christy organizations.[5] Charley Howard (1826-1895) was one of the first to play the part of an aged darky.[6]  Many imitated his success, and the impersonations of the legendary figure of "Old Black Joe" remained popular to the

[4] See Leavitt, *op. cit.*, p. 36; and Stone, *Personal Recollections*, p. 241.

[5] Rice, *Monarchs of Minstrelsy*, p. 52.

[6] *Ibid.*, p. 51.

present time. One of the last and best performers in these rôles of "Old Black Joe" was Johnny Healy, who played with the Field Minstrels almost to the last year of that organization's existence. Ben Cotton, who ran away from home in 1845 to join a theatre company, and who made his last appearance in Tony Pastor's Opera House in 1906 at the age of seventy-six, also achieved distinction by his characterizations of aged darkies. For many years, he had studied the real Negro type while running up and down the Mississippi on a river boat.[7]

L. V. H. Crosby was one of the first successful "middlemen" or interlocutors.[8]   John H. Carle (1825-1900) enjoyed considerable popularity in the middle of the last century, singing the comic song, "The Lively Old Flea," to banjo accompaniment.[9] John Washington Smith (1815-1877) sang his best known song, "Old Bob Ridley," in New Orleans, as early as 1849; and "Jim Along Josey," another typical early minstrel favorite is sometimes credited to Ned Harper.[10]   Dan Gardner, (1816-1880), another successful "Negro wench" actor, specialized on an impersonation of "Lucy Long."[11]   Joe Sweeney, whose real name was Joel Walker Sweeney (1813-

[7] Rice, *Monarchs of Minstrelsy*, p. 62.
[8] *Ibid.*, p. 50.
[9] *Ibid.*, p. 48.
[10] *Ibid.*, p. 24.
[11] *Ibid.*, p. 26.

1860), was one of the earliest banjo performers, and before the middle of the last century, he was traveling through the South, with his two brothers, as minstrel performers. Later on, he played with various circuses.[12] George Holland was a well-known wench impersonator with Christy and Wood's Minstrels in the late 1850's.[13] Frank Lynch, who starred in the preceding decade, was considered the "best representative of Ethiopian break-downs" in his time,[14] but his fame was overshadowed, at least temporarily, by the tremendous popularity of Jack Diamond, for some years the most popular dancer of Negro steps. As early as 1840, Diamond, then a mere boy, began to perform for P. T. Barnum in a variety bill at Vauxhall Garden, and later, the great promoter took his young dancer on a tour of Canada and the United States.[15] Diamond died in Philadelphia in 1857, at the early age of thirty-four. Riotous living had brought "one of the greatest delineators of Ethiopian dancing" to an untimely end, and Bryant's Minstrels had to donate the proceeds of one evening's performance so that the great dancer's final resting place might not remain unmarked.[16] Two of the best known colored dancers, who appeared with a number of minstrel companies

[12] Rice, *Monarchs of Minstrelsy*, p. 22.
[13] Hutton, *Curiosities of the American Stage*, p. 111.
[14] *Ibid.*
[15] Werner, *op. cit.*, pp. 40-41.
[16] *The New York Clipper*, November 7, 1857.

during the period from 1850 to 1880, were Horace Weston and Master Juba (William H. Lane).[17]

"Eph" Horn, another of the earliest minstrel stars and often described as "the Yorick of Negro Minstrelsy," was born in Philadelphia, in 1823. He made his first appearance before the public as a subject for a lecturer on mesmerism, a pseudo-science, in which the American public was greatly interested about the middle of the nineteenth century. Horn probably put on the burnt cork for the first time in 1840. He performed with various circuses and minstrel companies, at a salary which gradually mounted from $17 to $100 a week. In 1865, he played in England, starring in acts like "The Four Crows," the "Locomotive Nigger," and "Woman's Rights." Many of his best skits, like "Returned Volunteers," "The Shakers," and the "Stage-Struck Darkey," he wrote himself. He was said to have been very original and excruciatingly funny in his character sketches, and audiences never tired of his imitations of locomotives in motion and about to come to rest.[18]

Charles White was born in New York in 1821, and made his first appearance as an accordeon player. Early in the 'forties he organized The Kitchen Minstrels, opening at Palmer's Concert Room in New York City. Two years later, he opened his own theatre on the Bowery. He was

[17] Rice, *Monarchs of Minstrelsy,* pp. 46-48.
[18] Brown, *History of the American Stage,* pp. 182-183.

well-known as a Negro comedian, and, in later years,
owned and managed a number of theatres.[19]  Ben
Mallory, a member of the original Christy Minstrels,
ended his career as a circus rider.[20]  George Washington Moore, better known as "Pony" Moore because of his small size, was another of the early minstrel stars.  Born in 1825, he ran away from home
as a boy of sixteen, to join a circus.  Later, he traveled with a pantomime company.  In 1844, he made
his first appearance as a minstrel performer.  In
1859, he went to England, and in his later years,
was co-manager of a company of "Christys" at St.
James Hall in London.[21]  Cool White (John
Hodges) was one of the early interlocutors, and a
favorite for his portrayal of a Negro dandy and his
burlesques of Shakespeare.[22]  Sam S. Sanford, to
whom reference has already been made as one of the
greatest of the early minstrels, at one time owned
a number of theatres and several traveling companies.[23]

William P. Spaulding, born in Boston in 1836,
and Antonio (Tony) Pastor, born in New York in
1835, also belong to this group of early minstrel
favorites. The former made his first appearance as
a banjo player with George Christy's Minstrels in

[20] *Ibid.,* p. 232.
[21] *Ibid.,* pp. 250-251.
[22] Rice, *Monarchs of Minstrelsy,* p. 34.
[23] *Ibid.*

1856, in Savannah. During his long career, Spaulding traveled with many companies. When he retired from the burnt cork circle, he organized Spaulding Brothers' Bell Ringers, a very popular musical act in New York. Spaulding was exceedingly versatile, and played nearly every musical instrument. He was especially noted for his work on the bass bells.[24] Tony Pastor, as a boy, sang at temperance meetings. In 1846, he was a member of a minstrel troupe in Barnum's Museum, where he was associated with Charles White, Hall Robinson and other early favorites. The next year, Pastor joined Raymond and Waring's Menagerie, as a Negro performer. Later, he and his two brothers entered the circus business. In July, 1865, in association with Sam Sharpley, Pastor opened the Opera House in the Bowery which was to win him renown and fortune.[25]

Francis Leon, who made his début as a minstrel in Wood's Marble Hall of Minstrelsy on Broadway at the age of fourteen, was born in 1844. He began his career as a boy soprano, singing the soprano parts in a number of Masses in the Catholic church where he was a communicant. Leon is remembered mainly because of his association with Edwin Kelly, in Leon and Kelly's Minstrels. Kelly was born in Dublin, and had studied in London to become a sur-

[24] Brown, *History of the American Stage*, p. 345.
[25] *Ibid.*, pp. 277-278.

geon. But he had a fine tenor voice and an excellent stage presence, and early abandoned his medical studies to go on the stage in America. In 1866, in association with Leon, he fitted up the old Hope Chapel in New York City as a minstrel hall, and the company played there for three years, before leaving for a short engagement in London, England. His partner, Leon, who had a rich soprano voice and a very frail body, was admirably fitted for burlesquing the famous prima donnas of the day. He was generally billed as "The Only Leon," female impersonator.[26]

Harry Leslie, well-known as a tight rope walker, was born in East Troy, New York, in 1837. He made his first public appearance as a tambourine player with a minstrel company traveling in New England. Then he took his own organization on a tour of Canada. After a year's experience as owner of a New York dancing academy, he reëntered minstrelsy in 1857, as a member of Bryant's Minstrels. In 1868 and 1869, he was featured as harlequin in the pantomime company, "Humpty Dumpty." Leslie was a very versatile actor, and attracted special attention by his balloon ascensions and his feats as a tight-rope performer.[27] Barney Williams, before he became a player of Irish parts, had made something of a reputation as a "wench" impersonator.

[26] Brown, *History of the American Stage*, pp. 202-203, and Leavitt, *op. cit.*, p. 36.
[27] Brown, *History of the American Stage*, p. 217.

In the "hoe-down" dances, he would appear in a tawdry old gown of gaudy colors, with short and scanty skirts, from which frilled "panties" and huge shoes protruded.[28]

Dan Bryant was one of the greatest of the minstrel kings. His real name was Daniel Webster O'Brien. As a boy, he had worked as a baggage porter in hotels. Before the close of the 'forties, this young Irishman made his first appearance as a minstrel in New York. Bryant played with many companies, and in 1857, his own company opened in New York City. Ten years later, he took it to California. Dan Bryant's chief claim to fame rested upon his ability as a dancer of such favorites as "The Essence of Old Virginny," and "Shoo Fly." He had few rivals in "shaking up a grotesque essence." "Shoo Fly," a song and dance, usually was done with Dave Reed, an endman and performer with the bones who was so famous for his rendition of "Sally Come Up" and "Shoo Fly," that he became known as the "Sally Come Up Man."[29] Mert Sexton was a close rival of Bryant in these Negro dances.[30] Jerry (O'Brien) Bryant, the older of the Bryant brothers, was a comedian and endman, who had begun his minstrel career as a ballad singer. Besides playing with many American troupes, he ap-

[28] Logan, "The Ancestry of Brudder Bones," p. 698.
[29] Rice, *Monarchs of Minstrelsy*, pp. 87-88.
[30] *The New York Clipper*, November 5, 1859.

peared also in England and Australia. In 1857, with his brothers Dan and Neil, he founded Bryant's Minstrels. He made his last appearance in 1861.[31] Bryant's Minstrels were long remembered for their excellent delineations of the genuine Negro, and for their clever burlesques. Such skits as the burlesques of the "Carnival of Chivalry," as the "Carnival of Shovelry," or a Negro impersonation of Richard III, or the burlesque rendition of the anvil chorus, in which the company tapped the rhythm on huge anvils with little tack hammers, never failed to send the audiences of the 1850's and 1860's into gales of laughter.[32]

Lon Morris, business manager, first banjoist, and middleman for the famous Morris Brothers, Pell and Trowbridge's Minstrels of Boston, also was the author of dozens of banjo songs and Ethiopian pieces, like "Father John's Dream," "Five Miles Out of Town," "Ireland and Virginia," "Dusty Bob," "Purty Boy with the Glass Eye," "Shucking of the Corn," "Our Old Dog Has Broke His Leg," "On the Road to Brighton," etc. Billy Morris, another partner, was an endman and expert tambourinist, who sang with a very sweet voice such favorites as "Peter Gray" and "Ruben Wright," in the late 1850's. Johnny Pell of the same company,

---

[31] Rice, *Monarchs of Minstrelsy*, pp. 58-59.
[32] *The New York Clipper*, April 24, 1858; February 27, 1858; December 19, 1857.

played the other end with the bones; W. H. Brock-
way was the leading violinist of the troupe, and a
singer and a performer of wench parts in the afterpiece; and Dick Sliter did most of the dancing.[33]

J. W. McAndrews was known as "The Watermelon Man," a sketch which he did' for three decades. McAndrews had a full, rich voice, and a
perfect mastery of Negro talk. His act was an
actual reproduction of a darky whom he had encountered while on tour in Savannah, Georgia, in
1856. McAndrews followed the darky around until
he could imitate his manner and speech perfectly.
He even bought the garments of the old watermelon
peddler—a quaint old figure who went from place to
place, shouting at the top of his voice, with a small
donkey hitched to his cart. McAndrews played this
particular part until his death in 1899.[34]

William W. Newcomb began as a Negro dancer
with a circus. In 1851, while a member of Fellow's
Minstrels in New York, he invented and produced
the original "breakdown," called "The Essence of
Old Virginia," and his popular "Burlesque Lecture
on Woman's Rights." He also was known for his
stump speeches. Later on, he organized the Rumsey

[33] The complete roster of this company can be found in *The New
York Clipper*, February 19, 1859. For Matt Peel's Campbell Min-
strels, see *ibid.*, February 13, 1858, and for the roster of Bryant's
Minstrels, *ibid.*, February 28, 1857.

[34] Rice, *Monarchs of Minstrelsy*, p. 79; and Leavitt, *op. cit.*, p. 31.

and Newcomb Minstrels, a troupe which played with great success in the British Isles and on the continent of Europe, as well as in all parts of the United States. In Havana, the company gave forty-two concerts, with a profit of thirty thousand dollars. In 1868, Newcomb was forced to retire from the stage because of ill health.[35]

E. Freeman Dixey began his career at the age of eighteen, in Boston. He was noted as a bone player, and for his playing of wench roles. In 1862, he became the partner of Carncross, and thus Carncross and Dixey's Minstrels, one of the best minstrel organizations in the United States, was launched.[36] Thomas B. Dixon's (1847-1890) specialty was the old ballad "Sally in Our Alley."[37] Sam Hague was one of the rare examples of an English minstrel manager and clog dancer who came to the United States to follow his profession. He toured the country in the 1850's. While here, he organized a colored troupe, known as Hague's Georgia Minstrels, and took them to England. In 1866, he was the owner and manager of a mixed company of white and black performers playing in London.[38] J. E. Green ("Mocking Bird Green") achieved popularity by his singing and whistling of this old favorite.[39]

---

[35] Brown, *History of the American Stage*, pp. 262-263.
[36] Rice, *Monarchs of Minstrelsy*, p. 86.
[37] *Ibid.*, p. 198.
[38] Rice, *Monarchs of Minstrelsy*, p. 56.
[39] *Ibid.*, p. 86.

Willis Palmer Sweatnam did his first blackface act as a lad in the Western Museum in Cincinnati. The first minstrel company with which he was identified was a troupe on the show boat *Huron,* plying up and down the Little Miami Canal in Ohio.[40]  Later, he traveled the Wabash Canal on the show boat *Dixie.*[41]  In this connection, it is interesting to point out that G. R. Spaulding, a minstrel manager of the 'fifties and 'sixties, at one time owned four show boats, the *Floating Palace,* the *Banjo,* the *Gazelle,* and the *James Raymond,* and these boats stopped to give performances at most of the landings along the Mississippi and its tributaries.[42] In the same period, show boats like the *Cotton Blossom* and the *Water Queen* were plying the Ohio and its numerous branches, and Dave Reed's Minstrels, led by Johnny Booker, were performing daily in the concert room of the *James Raymond.* All these river boats were equipped with great calliopes, which could be heard for miles inland, and by which the eager patrons of the show boats were summoned to the local landings.

Another interesting character who devoted three years of his professional career to the minstrel stage was Ralph Keeler. Keeler began in Toledo, Ohio, as a dancer, at the age of eleven. Johnny Booker, a

[40] Rice, *Monarchs of Minstrelsy,* p. 179.
[41] Leavitt, *op. cit.,* p. 43.
[42] Rice, *op. cit.,* p. 23.

theatrical manager during the 1830's and after, and the author of two songs which were popular in his time, "Meet Johnny Booker in Bowling Green," and "Johnny Booker Help dis Nigger," discovered Keeler while the lad was dancing in a saloon. Booker himself was a minstrel actor, one of his best acts being "The Smoke-House Reel," in which he appeared with an old valise and umbrella. He ended his theatrical activities with a circus and menagerie.

At five dollars a week, Keeler began his career as a dancer of the "Juba," and the "Lucy Long." His costume consisted of flannel knee breeches, cheap lace, tarnished gold tinsel, a corked face and a wooly wig. Toledo hailed him as its infant prodigy. After a so-called "benefit" performance, in his home town, which the lad soon discovered was only a clever advertising trick to increase box office receipts for his manager, Keeler began traveling with "The Metropolitan Serenaders." When that organization failed, Keeler joined the smaller "Booker Troupe," with which he played in many parts of the west.

In his charmingly told *Vagabond Adventures* (Boston, 1872), Keeler paints an interesting picture of minstrelsy as it flourished before the middle of the last century. Booker's troupe made it a practice to stop at all state prisons along the way, and here the young dancer sang and danced for the prisoners, usually during the dinner hour. In small towns, where the show played but one performance, it was customary to conclude the evening's entertainment with a ball, "by particular request." While the performers were removing the burnt cork from their faces, the ushers removed the seats, and for an additional fee, the ladies and gentlemen of the audience were readmitted to the hall for the dance. At Cincinnati, Keeler joined "The Mitchells," a company headed by Mike Mitchell, until recently a member of Campbell's Minstrels. Here Keeler played at the largest hall in Cincinnati, and for a few days, he lived in unaccustomed luxury at the Gibson House, one of the town's best hotels. The company carried as its orchestra leader a young Italian who had been in grand opera in Havana, a German violinist, and three endmen in addition to Keeler. The troupe broke up in a small town in southern Ohio, and was in such financial straits that there was not enough cash on hand to get the company back to Cincinnati.

Keeler also played on *The Floating Palace,* a show boat pulled by a steamer along the rivers of the Middle West and South. Besides the minstrel company, this show boat carried a museum of ladies, dancing puppets, stuffed giraffes, and many wax figures. On the steam tug, *The Raymond,* there was a concert saloon in which minstrel shows were given. The two boats left Cincinnati for Wheeling with nearly a hundred performers and workmen on board, and from Wheeling, started down the Ohio, often making landings in two or three towns a day. Shows usually were given in the afternoon and evening, although morning performances were not uncommon. The boat proceeded down the Mississippi and the whole navigable lengths of the Cumberland and Tennessee rivers. A newspaper, known as *The Palace Journal,* was published in the museum for free distribution to the patrons of the show, and gingerbread, lemonade and brilliantly colored candies were distributed for advertising purposes. Frequently, fist fights and brawls occurred at the lawless backwoods landings, and one of the most important members of the company was a giant doorkeeper who guarded the entrance to the show boat. Indeed, every member of the company was armed, and might be called upon in emergencies. Many years later, Keeler abandoned his stage career for the field of journalism, and in 1873, he was sent by the *New York Tribune* to Cuba, as a special feature writer. In that island, torn by revolution and guerrilla warfare, Keeler mysteriously disappeared and no trace of him was ever found.[43]

Efforts to find reliable data on many other minstrels who played during the middle period in the

[43] See Ralph Keeler, *Vagabond Adventures* (Boston, 1872), pp. 101-220; Keeler, "Three Years as a Negro Minstrel," in *Atlantic Monthly,* XXIV, 71-85; and Hutton, *Curiosities of the American Stage,* pp. 107-108.

history of minstrelsy have proved unsuccessful. Only a few remain to be noted. Tom Christian, a member of Christy's New York company in the 1850's, was one of the first singers to introduce Tyrolean warbling and yodelling into the minstrel first part, and this type of singing quickly became a popular feature of minstrel concerts.[44]  Gustave Bideaux, an eccentric Frenchman, was a balladist of great reputation, and during the Civil War period, moved many a minstrel audience to tears by his rendition of "Dear Mother, I've Come Home to Die."

Queen and West were a well-known song and dance team in the late 1860's, following Thompson and Kerns, probably the first double blackface song and dance team on the minstrel stage.[45]  James Sanford and Charles Wilson, performers in the 1870's, were musical comedians, featuring comedy selections on the banjo and violin.[46]  "Marsh" Adams (Marshall Adams) who died in 1885, was said to have been the first to sing "Old Black Joe" in character.[47]  Washington Norton was a minstrel performer who went to England in 1861, played three months at the Royal Alhambra Palace in London, and later took a minstrel band to South Africa.[48]

[44] Rice, *Monarchs of Minstrelsy*, p. 23.
[45] *Ibid.*, pp. 133, 155.
[46] *Ibid.*, p. 152.
[47] *Ibid.*, p. 131.
[48] Brown, *History of the American Stage*, p. 267.

William Henry Rice, not related to "Daddy" Rice, was one of the best known minstrels for nearly a half century, and was particularly famous for his mimicry and impersonation of famous actors and singers, and for the clever way in which he mixed low comedy with well-known operatic selections. His second son, Edward Leroy Rice, was a minstrel manager, and a writer on American minstrelsy.[49] Among the great minstrel managers, William Arlington began life as a blacksmith, Cal Wagner as a locomotive fireman and engineer, and Charles Duprez as a tailor. Julia Gould probably deserves to be mentioned as one of the few women who appeared in blackface opera burlesques with minstrel companies in the 1850's and 1860's.[50]

As suggested in an earlier chapter, minstrelsy enjoyed tremendous popularity on the Pacific coast, immediately following the rush to California after the discovery of gold. The original San Francisco Minstrels, owned by Birch, Wambold, Bernard and Backus, were an interesting group. William Birch was born in Utica, New York, in 1831. At the age of thirteen, he made his first appearance as a minstrel performer. During his prime as a blackface actor, he starred as an endman and comedian. On the opposite end of the semi-circle sat Charles

[49] Rice, *Monarchs of Minstrelsy*, p. 163.
[50] *Ibid.*, p. 46.

Backus, son of a Rochester physician, who entered minstrelsy at the age of twenty-three. Birch had a bald head, a mild, light, slow, drawling voice with a soft rippling laugh. Backus was much heavier, had false teeth, a stentorian voice, a mouth extending from ear to ear, and a rapid fire delivery. Much of the comedy of the show depended on the contrast between the appearance and manner of these two comedians. Almost every evening, new and extemporaneous comedy was injected into the dialogue, by these clever endmen.[51] William Bernard, who once practiced law in San Francisco, served as interlocutor. David Wambold starred as a balladist. Born in New Jersey in 1836, and intended for the butcher trade, he first put on the burnt cork in 1849. As a member of various minstrel companies, he visited England, Belgium, France, Prussia, Austria, Italy and Hungary.[52]

Other favorites of the Pacific coast audiences were Joe Murphy and Fred Sprung. The former began his career as a bone player and singer at auctions and cheap entertainments in San Francisco, and later became the champion bone player of the west coast. The latter was a native of Germany, an excellent basso and a successful interlocutor, with much experience as a singer with the Mississippi

[51] See *Francis Wilson's Life of Himself*, p. 50.
[52] Brown, *History of the American Stage*, p. 376; Leavitt, *op. cit.* pp. 34-35.

River Boat Minstrels. Murphy later became an imitator of English comedians, and in one of his own plays, called "Help," impersonated a Chinaman, a Negro, an Irishman, and a German. He ended his stage career as an Irish comedian. Johnny de Angeles, father of the better known Jefferson de Angeles, was for some years an endman in San Francisco. Dick Sands and Billy Ashcraft were the first clog dancers of note on the west coast, and Johnny Tuers was the champion flat foot dancer. Walter Bray left the legitimate stage in the 1860's to play blackface parts, and was especially successful in burlesques of Shakespeare's plays. Besides Wambold, Henry Herbert, Tom Casselli, Tommy Bree, and J. G. Russell were the most popular ballad singers in early San Francisco. The last named apparently was traveling under an assumed name, because of an encounter with the law in the East. His rich baritone was featured in sentimental ballads like "You and I," and "We Parted by the Riverside."[53]

Billy Emerson was the greatest San Francisco minstrel favorite in the 1870's and 1880's. He was an all-round performer, a good dancer, and a singer with a voice of unusual range. Among his most famous songs were "The Big Sunflower," "Love Among the Roses," "The Yaller Gal That Looked

[53] See E. T. Sawyer, "Old-Time Minstrels of San Francisco," pp. 5-8.

at Me," "Tassels on Her Boots," "Mary Kelley's Beau," and "Nicodemus Johnson." Emerson, whose real name was William Emerson Redmond, was in the minstrel business since the middle of the nineteenth century. In 1873, he toured Australia. He made large salaries, but wasted his money in gambling, horse races, and the stock market, and died in poverty in 1902. One of America's greatest actors considered Emerson a real genius. Skits like his "Hungry Jake," were earnest, yet droll portrayals of the Negro type, and were done with rare artistry.[54]

R. M. Hooley, who came to the United States from Ireland and played with Christy's Minstrels, organized Hooley and Campbell's Minstrels in 1860. He built several minstrel theatres and in 1876 was part owner of Rice and Hooley's Minstrels.[55] J. W. Raynor was another of Ireland's contributions to the American minstrel stage.[56] Fred Wilson was a clog dancer with Thayer's and Bryant's Minstrels and later had a company of his own.[57] Guy Brothers' Minstrels were organized by George Guy and his six talented sons.[58] J. Unsworth, who played regularly with Bryant's Minstrels in the 1850's, was one

[54] See *Francis Wilson's Life*, pp. 48-50.
[55] Rice, *Monarchs of Minstrelsy*, p. 38.
[56] *Ibid.*, p. 39.
[57] *Ibid.*, p. 55.
[58] *Ibid.*, p. 36.

of the greatest eccentric banjo players of all time and a clever monologist.[59] Sam Price was well known for his old Negro act, "Haunted House," and in the 1860's starred as an endman with Matt Peel's Minstrels.[60]

Matt Peel, after whom the show was named, died in Buffalo, in May, 1859, playing minstrel parts until two days before his death, at the age of twenty-nine years. Thousands viewed the remains of the minstrel king, passing by the coffin which stood on the sidewalk of a prominent New York street in order to give the huge crowds an opportunity to pay their respects to the popular entertainer. Among the pallbearers were such minstrel celebrities as Emmett, the three Bryants, Prendergast, E. P. Christy, Charley White, James Carroll, E. H. Winchell and John Sivori. Peel was long remembered as the eccentric comedian who coined many of the popular sayings of the late 'fifties.[61]

Johnny Allen, whose real name was George Erb, made his first blackface appearance in 1861, and after a number of years in minstrelsy, became a German comedian, playing popular "Schneider" rôles during the decades of the preceding century, when there was a heavy German immigration.[62] The

[59] *The New York Clipper,* November 6, 1858.
[60] Rice, *Monarchs of Minstrelsy,* p. 38.
[61] *The New York Clipper,* May 14, 1859.
[62] Rice, *Monarchs of Minstrelsy,* p. 175.

Campbell family had four representatives on the minstrel stage.[63]   T. B. Prendergast, already mentioned in connection with the Campbell and other minstrels, was a popular female impersonator. Henry Woodson (John Archer Shields) played "aged darkey" rôles, and gave a rendition of the song, "That Old Gray Mule of Mine," which became a minstrel classic.[64]   Harrigan and Hart, the most famous Irish comedians in the 1870's, started as ballad singers with the minstrels, and the latter was called "the best 'genteel wench' that ever trod the boards."   G. Swayne Buckley, once head of Buckley's Serenaders, featured a musical specialty, "Music on the Brain," in which he not only played a great array of instruments, but several of them at once.[65]

Colonel Jack Haverly should be remembered as the founder of the modern large scale minstrel show. Haverly was not a performer himself, but a very resourceful organizer and manager.   He began his career as a "baggage smasher."   Then he became the owner of a little variety theatre in Toledo.   In 1864, he entered the minstrel business.   When he led his minstrel parades through the streets, he looked more like a minister of the gospel than a show-

[63] Leavitt, op. cit., p. 28.
[64] Rice, op. cit., p. 238.
[65] Tompkins, History of the Boston Theatre, 1854-1901 (Boston, 1908), pp. 177-178.

man. In 1878, he sent out Haverly's Mastodon Minstrels—"Forty—Count 'em—Forty." The number of performers steadily grew to nearly a hundred. Haverly made and lost several fortunes during his career as owner of many companies and as manager of a chain of theatres. Some of his companies he took to Great Britain and Germany. Many minstrel stars had some of their earliest engagements with one of Haverly's organizations. This list would include Billy Emerson, Hughey Dougherty, Milton G. Barlow, Luke Schoolcraft, West, and Primrose.

One of the most interesting chapters in the history of the theatre in the United States might be written around the great number of first-class actors and performers who got their first theatrical experience in minstrelsy. The great tragedian, Edwin Booth, gave a blackface performance in 1850, at Belair, Maryland, singing a number of Negro melodies to banjo and bone accompaniment.[66] Joseph Jefferson, as a four year old child, appeared with "Daddy" Rice in a "Jim Crow" performance.[67] Edwin Forrest and John S. Clarke blacked up for Negro parts,[68] although they were never members of a

[66] Hutton, *Curiosities of the American Stage*, p. 106; Rice, *op. cit.*, p. 91.

[67] Lewis C. Strang, *Players and Plays of the Last Quarter Century* (Boston, 1903), I, 262.

[68] Quinn, *op. cit.*, p. 334.

minstrel troupe.  The inimitable P. T. Barnum put
on the burnt-cork in Camden, South Carolina, when
his Negro singer left the troupe with which he was
touring the South by means of wagons, horses, and
canvas tents; and the "Prince of Humbugs" regularly sang such early favorites as "Zip Coon," "The
Raccoon Hunt," and "Gittin' Up Stairs" until he
could hire another Negro singer and dancer, for
Barnum's Grand Scientific and Musical Theatre.[69]

Patrick S. Gilmore, famous band leader, was a
member of Ordway's Aeolians and at one time sat
on the end, playing a tambourine.[70]  Chauncey Olcott, famous as an actor and singer in Irish romantic
plays, began his career in the blackface ranks, as
manager and tenor of Emerson's Minstrels on the
Pacific coast, and as a player in the well-known
Carncross Minstrel Company in Philadelphia.[71]
Three members of the Frohman family, successful
theatrical producers, began their careers as managers and advance agents for minstrel companies in
the 1870's.[72]  Francis Wilson, one of America's
greatest actors of the present generation, was a circus performer and a minstrel in the early years of
his theatrical life, and a member of the Mackin and

---

[69] Werner, *op. cit.*, pp. 38-39.
[70] Rice, *Monarchs of Minstrelsy*, p. 60.
[71] *Munsey's Magazine*, XX, 961-962.
[72] Rice, *Monarchs of Minstrelsy*, p. 264.

Wilson song and dance team, until he was twenty-three years of age.[73]

George Frothingham, the basso who created the rôle of Friar Tuck in *Robin Hood* and sang this rôle over three thousand times, was for many years in the minstrels.[74] Gus Sun, himself a juggler and then head of a well-established vaudeville circuit, started with Sun Brothers' Circus and soon thereafter created the Gus Sun Minstrels.[75] Charles J. Ross, well known at the close of the last century as a great mimic, a star in Weber and Fields burlesque company, and an imitator of Faversham, Southern, and Gillette, started with "nigger acts."[76] Other stars of recent times who either blacked up or were associated with minstrel companies in earlier days are Dave Montgomery and Fred Stone, Raymond Hitchcock, Joseph Cawthorn, Maclyn Arbuckle, De Wolf Hopper, Nat Goodwin, Eddie Foy, Sam Bernard, George M. Cohan, Lew Fields, Willie Collier, and Joe Weber.

Nat Goodwin, in 1876, was doing a specialty of imitations with Haverly's Minstrels in Chicago.[77] The first joint appearance of Montgomery and Stone was with a minstrel company, in New Or-

[73] *Francis Wilson's Life of Himself,* pp. 36-45.

[74] Rice, *op. cit.,* p. 174.

[75] *Ibid.,* pp. 334-335; and *The New York Clipper,* December 28, 1901.

[76] *Munsey's Magazine,* XIX, 933.

[77] Rice, *Monarchs of Minstrelsy,* p. 268.

leans, in 1895.[78] George M. Cohan's father played with Campbell and Huntley's Minstrels in 1868, as a blackface tambourine performer.[79] John Philip Sousa, "the March King," was a member of Simmons and Slocum's Minstrels when Al G. Field was serving his apprenticeship with that company, and Dan Rice, one of the most famous circus clowns America has produced, began as a minstrel.[80] Eddie Leonard was a member of Haverly's, Cohan and Harris, Dockstader's and Primrose and West's shows, and Al Jolson, who still resorts to burnt cork in his musical comedy and film performances, was discovered by Lew Dockstader, and appeared with the latter's minstrel company.[81] J. J. Corbett, "Gentleman Jim," equally well known as a champion pugilist and as an actor, once served as interlocutor in George Evans' Minstrels. The La Barre Brothers, leading contortionists and acrobats with many minstrel organizations, celebrated the fiftieth anniversary of their first performance, in January, 1929. Another of the veterans, still living, is Major Miles Gorman, a minstrel and vaudeville performer for nearly sixty years, who began trouping at the age of eight, with the Buckley Minstrels in Boston.[82]

[78] Rice, *Monarchs of Minstrelsy*, p. 342.
[79] *Ibid.*, p. 203.
[80] Al G. Field, "The History of Minstrelsy," p. 63.
[81] Rice, *op. cit.*, pp. 363-364.
[82] *The Billboard*, May 18, 1929; June 8, 1929.

The drum majors of the minstrel bands were great attractions with the minstrel troupes on tour, and for a time, before the novelty wore off, expert tossers of the baton, who could juggle the beribboned stick and head the band on parade, were in great demand. The minstrels produced a great array of popular drum majors. Among them were experts like Owen A. Brady, for many years with Vogel's Big City Minstrels, Fred (Major) Smith with W. H. West's Minstrels, Joe Egan of Lew Dockstader's company, Teddy Roberts of Cohan and Harris' Honey Boy Evans Minstrels, Johnny Whalen of the Ward and Vokes Show, Jack Cullen of Calhoun-Chase-Western Minstrels, and Jimmie Devland, long with Al G. Field.[83]

Some of the greatest stars in minstrelsy appeared during the declining years of the profession. Field, Dockstader, Evans, Primrose, O'Brien, Thatcher, and West, although comparatively late comers in the history of blackface entertainment, have won a permanent place in the annals of minstrelsy alongside the greatest stars of earlier days.

Neil O'Brien did not begin his career until 1889. He always played the rôle of a real, roustabout, eccentric Southern darky, with very little caricaturing of the part, and he has been called by some minstrel managers of long experience "the greatest of

[83] See *The Billboard*, June 29, 1929, p. 37.

the moderns." O'Brien played in various companies, like Haverly's, Primrose and Dockstader's, and Field's minstrels, as endman and singer of his own comedy songs, before he launched his own show. Intermittently, he appeared in vaudeville.[84] In the spring of 1929, O'Brien was teaming with James J. Corbett in vaudeville. Frank Dumont wrote probably more songs, jokes, and afterpieces for minstrel shows than any other performer or producer. For years he owned and managed the old Eleventh Street Opera House in Philadelphia, a playhouse devoted to minstrelsy exclusively for over half a century. The final curtain was rung down in the spring of 1911.[85] George Thatcher made his début at the New Idea Concert Hall in Baltimore in 1865, as a song and dance man. He was one of the greatest monologists in modern minstrelsy, and played with many companies before he was associated with Primrose and West and Dockstader, or managed his own organization.[86]

James McIntyre, born in 1857, and Thomas K. Heath, born in 1853, probably the most famous team minstrelsy has produced, formed their partnership in 1874. For some years, they appeared with circuses and variety shows. In 1876, they were head-

[84] Rice, *Monarchs of Minstrelsy*, pp. 330-331; Leavitt, *op. cit.*, pp. 38-46.

[85] Leavitt, *op. cit.*, pp. 47-48.

[86] *Ibid.*, p. 42.

liners at the old Theatre Comique at St. Louis, at what was then one of the largest salaries paid to burnt cork artists.[87]  In 1878, they organized the McIntyre and Heath Minstrels.  Their most famous act probably was "The Georgia Minstrels," although they have appeared in a great variety of performances.  In 1906, this blackface team was featured in the musical extravaganza, called the *Ham Tree,* and in 1909, they played in *In Hayti.*  During their long career, they have also been associated with Lew Dockstader and with the comedy team of Weber and Fields.  In 1924, the venerable minstrel team celebrated the fiftieth anniversary of their partnership.  They were still playing blackface, but in vaudeville.  In 1928, they appeared with a Shubert production, "Headin' South," as the premier burnt cork comedians of the play.[88]

George Evans, "Honey Boy" Evans as he was called because he wrote the popular favorite, "I'll Be True to My Honey Boy," was born in 1870.  He made his first appearance with a quartette in Canton, Ohio, in 1891.  For several months he traveled with medicine shows.  His first minstrel engagement was with Haverly in Chicago, in 1892.  Thereafter, he starred with Cleveland's, and Primrose and West's Minstrels, in vaudeville as a comedian and

[87] *The New York Clipper,* December 28, 1901.
[88] Rice, *Monarchs of Minstrelsy,* pp. 255-262.

singer, and as a white face performer in musical comedies.  In 1908, he was the star of Cohan and Harris' revival of minstrelsy at Atlantic City.  In 1910, he became the owner of a minstrel show. Evans died in 1915.  His vaudeville act, "The Seven Honey Boys," was long a favorite with the theatre-going public.  Besides the song which gave him his stage name, "Honey Boy" Evans wrote popular hits like "Standing on the Corner, Didn't Mean No Harm," "Come Take a Trip in My Airship," "In the Good Old Summertime," and "Down Where the Watermelon Grows."[89]

George H. Primrose, whose real name was De-laney, was born in London, Canada, and began his stage career as a juvenile clog dancer, in 1867, with McFarland's Minstrels in Detroit.  Later, he danced in a Buffalo music hall, five times a day, for five dollars a week.  He became famous as one of the greatest soft shoe dancers of all time, although he also was successful as a singer.  After appearing with various minstrel companies and circuses, he formed a partnership with William H. West, and Primrose and West's Minstrels were on the road for thirty years.  Later Primrose was associated with George Thatcher and Lew Dockstader, and also played several seasons of vaudeville.  Indeed, Prim-rose and Dockstader were among the last minstrels

[89] Rice, *Monarchs of Minstrelsy*, p. 339.

to tour the large cities. When that partnership dissolved, commented the South Bend *Tribune,* "the curtain came down on a form of entertainment peculiarly American, about which linger some of the sweetest memories of the stage."[90]  Primrose died in San Diego, California, in 1919, at the age of sixty-six years.

Lew Dockstader, whose real name was George Alfred Clapp, was born in Hartford, Connecticut, in 1856. His first appearance was with an amateur show in his home town, in a song and dance act. His first professional engagement was at Springfield, Massachusetts, as a member of Harry Bloodgood's Comic Alliance troupe. In 1877, Dockstader played in San Francisco, featuring a song and dance called "Peter, You're in Luck This Morning." In 1878, he returned to New York, to form an alliance with Charles Dockstader, and the team became known as Dockstader Brothers. It was then that Lew adopted the name which he made famous in the history of minstrelsy. Dockstader played blackface throughout his long career. In 1886, after having played in many variety houses and minstrel companies, Dockstader opened his own show in New York City, where it ran for three years.

The great minstrel king's programs as presented in his own playhouse week after week in the season

[90] Quoted in "Passing of the Minstrels," *The Literary Digest,* August 16, 1919, pp. 28-29.

of 1887 throw considerable light on Dockstader's activities as a director and organizer of minstrel productions, as they reveal also his own peculiar talent for burlesque and mimicry. In January, 1887, Dockstader's company completed its second hundred consecutive performances in New York. "How the Christy's of old would stare at such perfect performances," commented the *New York Mirror*.[91] But the performance was quite different from the minstrel shows of three or four decades ago. Dockstader's first part represented the Knickerbocker Club, and the actors were attired in the finest silk stockings, pumps, and white waistcoats. The first part still resembled the older programs. One week Dockstader featured a revival of Stephen C. Foster's famous songs; at another time, the first part was built largely around the songs of well-known German composers, and songs of Scotland. In December, 1887, Frank Howard, composer of such popular ballads as "Sweet Heather Bells," "When the Robins Nest Again," "Sweet Alpine Roses," "Only a Pansy Blossom," and "Only a Blue Bell," was added to the company. The program usually included a banjo number, and scenes from Southern plantations.

Dockstader himself was famous for his topical songs, and his clever, up-to-the-minute burlesques. Among his song hits of the 1887 season in New York

[91] Quoted in *New York Times*, January 9, 1887.

were "Never in the Wide, Wide World," "I Doubt
If It Ever Occurs," "Tootsie Wootsie," and "Dan-
ger Ahead." One of his most successful tricks was
burlesquing plays and actors appearing simultaneously in other New York theatres. When "Jim
the Penman" was produced at the Madison Square
Theatre, Dockstader introduced the burlesque, "Jim,
the Pieman." Because Theodore Thomas was ex-
periencing considerable trouble with his grand opera
ventures in New York, Dockstader produced a pantomime, an operatic finale entitled, "Thomas Much-
Mad, Eh! or National Opera Troubles." In February, 1887, he satirized the new mind-reading fad,
and presented himself as a mindreader who had appeared before all "the bald heads" of Europe. Again
Dockstader presented a burlesque, "Harbor Lights,"
in which he acted the part of a lieutenant who saved
the United States Navy from being annihilated by a
collision with the New York harbor lights. On another occasion, he concocted a droll afterpiece called
"The Fall of Babylon." We can only guess at its
nature from the comment of the *Times* reviewer
who wrote that Dockstader displayed "greater
knowledge of local politics than ever before." The
following week, Dockstader added a sketch dealing
with President Cleveland's western tour. This he
followed with a long and witty elucidation of the

prodigious problem whether Shakespeare or Bacon wrote the plays.

For the week of November 13, 1887, Dockstader appeared in "Black Faust," as Splinter, the Doctor's Boy, and advertised that Irving was outdone and Terry discouraged by his excellent performance. Irving was at the time starring in New York in *Faust*. The first scene showed Faust in his laboratory perfecting a bunion cure, and "The Messenger Boy's Chorus" was introduced as a burlesque of the famous "Soldiers' Chorus." Among Dockstader's best known sketches were "The Country School Scholar" and "Modern Mother Goose." When Josef Hofman, the boy pianist, made his début at the Metropolitan Opera House, Dockstader hastily added a boy pianist to his company and proceeded to burlesque Hofman's concerts. A travesty on "She," a play which had been running for weeks at Niblo's Theatre, was introduced by the following cablegram,

Lew Dockstader, Esq.

I hereby authorize you to burlesque "She" in your theatre. If she won't burlesque, discharge her.

HIDER RAGGARD.

*Henrietta,* and the *Taming of the Shrew,* were burlesqued, as well as "Willie Buffalo's Wildest West"; and *Ernimie* playing at the Casino, was presented as "Our Minnie." One of Dockstader's most successful monologues was "On Misfits," which he gave for the benefit of the Actors' Fund in 1887.[92] Another was "Election Day—or Fun at the Pools."

A typical Dockstader program for the fall season of 1887 follows:

### First Part

Overture—"Ruddigore" (Sullivan)..Dockstader's Minstrels
Bass Solo—Bedouin Love Song.......Henry W. Frillman
Baritone Solo—The Guiding Light (Henry)..Cortis Dalton
Topical Song—"Never in the Wide, Wide World"
    (Kidder).......................Lew Dockstader
Alto Solo—"Fold Those Little Hands in Prayer"
    (Wegefarth).............................R. José
Comic Song—"Simply Nothing at All" (Rankin)
                          Carl Rankin
Tenor Solo—"Sweet Days of Old" (Mullaly)
                           W. H. Reiger
   "The Coarsehair or The Northerland Sisters."

### Second Part

Edwin French and his Banjo.
Cleveland's Trip—Mr. Rankin as President Cleveland.
"The Arabian Nights, or Fun on the Old Homestead"
    (Franks, Marign, Perry, and Magrew)
Geo. H. Wood—"the somewhat different comedian."
The Fall of New Babylon—All comedians and The New
    Babylonian Ballet.[93]

[92] See *New York Times,* January 18, 23; February 22; February 6, 8, 15; November 13; December 4, 11; December 13, 18, 26, 1887; January 2, 10, 16, 20, 1887; October 3, 4, 9, 16, 1887; November 6, 1887.
[93] *New York Times,* October 23, 1887. Frillman, and his son, who traveled with the Field Minstrels, were two of minstrelsy's greatest bassos.

In 1888, Dockstader's Minstrels made their first Boston appearance, and met with immediate success. Besides Dockstader, who easily was the most popular member of the company, Richard J. José was enthusiastically received. José had come to the United States from England, as an orphan. He had a magnificent tenor voice, almost like an alto, and sang such old favorites as "Silver Threads Among the Gold," "I Love You in the Same Old Way," and "With All Her Faults I Love Her Still."[94] Late in 1889, Dockstader appeared in monologues with a vaudeville company at the Academy of Music in Philadelphia.[95] Thereafter, for two years, he was associated with Primrose and West, and then he joined George Thatcher's Minstrels. Thereupon he organized another company of his own. Intermittently, he played in vaudeville.

As has been said, Dockstader was specially famous for his monologues, and his ability to burlesque the performances of others. His "take-off" of President Roosevelt was one of his most excellent bits. One reason for his great popularity was his ability to introduce the latest local gossip in his monologues. So rapidly did he pick up the news in each locality that it was generally believed that he maintained scouts in each city to inform him of the latest events. In 1902, he appeared in a timely new

[94] Tompkins, *op. cit.*, pp. 359, 360, 365.
[95] *Philadelphia Press*, December 29, 1889.

monologue, "A Trip to the North Pole."[96]  Dockstader generally appeared for his monologue clad in
monstrous coat and huge shoes, and the moment he
walked upon the stage, his make-up was enough to
set off gales of laughter.   He also was extremely
skillful in parodying popular songs.   Under Dockstader's watchful eye many a present-day musical
comedy star received his first training for the stage.
Dockstader died in 1924, and with him minstrelsy
lost one of the last of the great delineators of Negro
character.[97]

George R. Guy has the distinction of being the
oldest active minstrel man, with a record of sixty-
six years in the burnt cork profession.  George Wilson and Willis P. Sweatnam are his seniors, but they
are no longer on the road.  George Guy was born in
the decade when Dan Emmett gave "Dixie" to the
American public.  He taught his six talented sons
all the tricks of the minstrel business, and two of
them, George Jr. and Willie, made their first blackface appearance before they were ten years old, and
claim to have done the first boy and "girl" blackface
specialty known to true American minstrelsy.  After
some experience with circuses and a tour of the
British Isles, George R. Guy and his six sons organized Guy Brothers' Mighty Minstrels.   The
various members of the family sang, danced, played

[96] *The New York Clipper*, February 8, 1902.
[97] Rice, *Monarchs of Minstrelsy*, p. 274.

tambos, bones, and musical instruments, and did acrobatic stunts, besides "doubling" in the band and orchestra. At one time, the company had thirty-eight performers, but the Guy family always played the key positions. George R. Guy, now seventy-three years of age, still does bone solos, blackface comedy, turns out for parades, and acts as a minstrel manager. He has an unshakable faith in the ultimate revival of American minstrelsy.[98]

Al G. Field, "the Dean of American Minstrelsy," was the last of the great producers of minstrel shows, and for over forty-one years, The Al G. Field Greater Minstrels toured the United States. Alfred Griffith Hatfield was born in Leesburg, Lowden County, Virginia, on November 7, 1848. While attending school in western Pennsylvania, to which his parents had moved, he began to show an interest in theatrical productions. In his charming autobiography, *Watch Yourself Go By* (Columbus, Ohio, 1912), he relates that he saw his first minstrel performance in a side-show connected with a circus, playing in Brownsville, Pennsylvania. The company, consisting of seven performers, clad in shirts and trousers made of bed-ticking, was advertised as "Christy's Original Minstrels."

Field, as a schoolboy, gave his first show in the little red brick school house in Brownsville. A

[98] See Earl Chapin May, "George R. Guy," in the *New York Herald Tribune*, July 14, 1929.

farmer in the neighborhood loaned the lumber and helped build the platform, while Field himself printed the show bill in the printing shop where he was employed. The advertisement announced "Hatfield and Storey's Alabama Minstrels—Red Stone School House—Early Candle Light." The admission was twenty-five cents for adults and half price for children. Field then began barnstorming with various minstrel troupes. The first, known as the Great Benedict Minstrels, traveled to all the oil towns of Pennsylvania, and played at Pithole, Rouseville, Petroleum Center, and Parker's Landing at a time when the local "opera houses" were sheds, with the audiences standing outside to listen. One of these companies, which followed the practice of sending one of its members through the town, ringing a bell, to announce the performance, finally was stranded in West Virginia. Field also traveled with an organization showing a panorama of Bunyan's *Pilgrim's Progress,* playing the part of Evangelist, at fifty dollars a month. With Thayer and Noyes' Great American Circus, Field worked as a song and dance man in the "concert" at fifteen dollars a week, and appeared in a tumbling act in the circus ring, clad in pink tights with spangled trimmings. Early in his career, he dropped the first syllable of his family name, probably because the shorter name had certain advantages from the point of view of billboard advertising, and in 1881, by action of the Franklin County Probate Court (Ohio), his name was legally changed to Al G. Field.

In 1875, Field's father moved to Columbus, Ohio, where he opened a contracting paint shop. Much of his work was done for Sells Brothers' Circus, an organization then located in Chillicothe. Al G. found employment as a "concert" musician and clown in Sells' Circus. He also played with Simmons and Slocum's Minstrels, and was offered a place with a company of Haverly Minstrels, about to leave for a tour of Europe. On another occasion, Field toured Texas with a wagon show. He also was associated with Sharply, Sheridan, Mack and Day's Minstrels, and just prior to the organization of his own company, was manager of a circus.

In 1886, Field organized the show which brought him fame and which was destined to remain in existence for forty-one years, the longest record established by any traveling minstrel organization. His first performance was given on October 6, at Marion, Ohio, with a company of twenty-seven. Each season thereafter, the show grew in size and splendor until it was the most elaborate and expensive minstrel show in existence. The Field Minstrels were the first to carry an entire stage setting and complete scenery, and the first to build and operate special railway cars to transport the person-

nel and equipment of the show. Field personally
wrote all his productions, and directed the rehearsals.
While on tour, he kept a scrap book in which he
carefully entered all sorts of local items, and from
this scrap book he often wrote the sketches and
afterpieces for his show. For many years, Field
took an active part in the performance, usually in
blackface, sometimes as an endman, sometimes as
a monologist, or sometimes as a companion to the
premier comedian.

Many recent minstrel and other theatrical performers were developed in the Field company.
"Lassus" White, Neil O'Brien, Bert Swor, and
"Doc" Quigley appeared with Field early in their
careers. Quigley, a song and dance man whose specialty was grotesque Negro dances, had the unique
distinction of spending his entire professional career
with the Al G. Field Minstrels. Bert Swor, one of
the best of the present-day minstrels, is a graduate
of the medicine show school and trouped several seasons with "Doc" C. J. Clifton who dispensed "Herbs
of Health" and pulled teeth. He began in the minstrel business proper with Haverly, played in stock
and vaudeville, and then became the premier endman
of the Field organization. Three brothers followed
Swor into the minstrel business. Billy Beard, "the
Party from the South," and the dancer, Johnny
Dove, also were associated with Field, and John W.

Vogel, a non-acting manager with a long experience in the circus and minstrel business, was Field's manager for seven years.

The Field minstrel season usually ran forty-six weeks, and took the show through the South and into many of the leading cities of the Middle Atlantic and Middle West sections. Field was one of the few minstrels who became wealthy through his theatrical ventures. He accumulated a substantial fortune, owned considerable real estate in his home city of Columbus, was a director of one of its large banks, and the owner of a beautiful country place known as "Maple Villa." Al G. Field died on April 3, 1921, one of the most highly regarded citizens of central Ohio, and a leader in many civic and charitable enterprises. He was buried in Greenlawn Cemetery, by the Knights Templars to which he belonged. The show which had carried his name throughout the nation closed in Cincinnati, in 1928. It was the last of the great professional minstrel companies.

# INDEX

[ 259 ]

## DATE DUE

| FE 29 '64 | | | |
|-----------|---|---|---|
| MY 1 7 '68 | | | |
| MY 2 1 '68 | | | |
| JA 24 '69 | | | |
| FE 7 '69 | | | |
| | | | |
| | | | |
| | | | |
| | | | |
| | | | |
| | | | |
| | | | |
| | | | |
| | | | |
| | | | |
| GAYLORD | | | PRINTED IN U.S.A. |

9 781013 702846